"Three words: I can't even. As a proud friend and follower of Rachel on Instagram (and IRL, of course), I was fully aware of her magical abilities to effortlessly whip up healthy versions of all of our nostalgic comfort foods and desserts. With *Just the Good Stuff*, she takes it to a whole new level. These recipes are inventive and inspirational, and they combine flavors in a way that you wouldn't think to, such as her Zesty Jalapeño Meatloaf. While reading this book, you'll feel like you've been invited into Rachel's home for a meal or sweet treat. Rachel makes you want to cozy up on the couch with little bites and invite your friends over for a sit-down dinner all at the same time. Whether a snack sesh featuring Dark Chocolate Nutty Puppy Chow or a meal-prep night with Sunday Roasted Chicken by Jord, you'll have endless cooking ideas in *Just the Good Stuff*."

—**Ali Maffucci,** *New York Times* bestselling cookbook author and founder of *Inspiralized*

"Rachel Mansfield turns healthy eating into an attainable and enjoyable experience with a beautiful collection of recipes that are simple to create yet complex enough in flavor that eating them makes you wonder what's been holding you back from the kitchen in the first place. Not only will you learn why you should fuel your body with certain foods, you'll learn how to translate these healthy ingredients into new favorite dishes as well as ones you have loved throughout your life."

—**Dr. Will Cole,** leading functional medicine expert and bestselling author of *The Inflammation Spectrum* and *Ketotarian*

"These recipes are the perfect mix of classic, emotion-tugging comfort food made healthy and innovative flavor combinations that stoke excitement about just how good healthy food can taste. While Rachel's baked goods are always drool-inspiring (the Maple Bacon Banana Nut Loaf might be the best banana bread I've ever had), the savory items shine as well. Enchilada Pie, in the sweetly community-building Gatherings section, is a new classic, and the crispy avocado tacos will win any #tacotuesday. Rachel's personality is as winning as her food—flipping through feels like talking to your cool best friend. The genius inclusion of shopping lists and meal-prep guides will make healthy eating easy for even total novices."

—**Liz Moody,** author of *Healthier Together* and host of the *Healthier Together* podcast

"*Just the Good Stuff* highlights how much there is to love about consuming real foods. With vulnerability and creativity, Rachel brings together recipes and stories that inspire us to use food as therapy every day. More than that, this book teaches us to embrace who we are in our journey to finding true self-love."

—**Priscilla Tsai,** founder and CEO of cocokind

"In *Just the Good Stuff*, Rachel creates recipes that are gluten-free, dairy-free, and deliciously vibrant. Her Crunchy Tahini Chocolate Grain-Free Granola and Paleo Everything Bagel Bread are just two of the many recipes you'll crave over and over again. Plus, having a guide to prepping food for the week, this book has you covered for all aspects of eating."

—**Frank Lipman, MD,** bestselling author of *The New Health Rules* and *How to Be Well*

100+ Guilt-Free Recipes to
Satisfy All Your Cravings

**GLUTEN-FREE, PALEO-FRIENDLY,
AND WITHOUT REFINED SUGAR**

just the good stuff

Rachel Mansfield

Photographs by
Aubrie Pick

Clarkson Potter/Publishers
New York

To my Ezra, you have made me the luckiest mama in the world. I love you to the moon and back—with tons of banana bread, snuggles, and stroller walks in between.

contents

food as therapy

my philosophy in the kitchen

My simple philosophy of eating *real food* is the culmination of years of yo-yo dieting and seeing my weight fluctuate like crazy. It has been an uphill battle for the past twenty-nine years, but I am finally in a place with both food and my body that makes me happy—and boy, does it feel good. I kicked calorie counting to the curb and ditched fat-free diet foods and fads. Now, I focus on what my body wants and what foods make it feel its best. To me, that means taking all the comfort foods I crave—pancakes, cookies, pierogis, pad Thai, burgers—and reinventing them with healthy, flavorful ingredients that make me feel great. I love sneaking in nutritious and wholesome ingredients like collagen peptides for an extra boost, and there is no doubt I get giddy over a good grass-fed burger with sliced

avocado, plus some coconut milk–based ice cream for dessert—just don't forget the nut butter drizzle and a sprinkle of crushed dark chocolate! Eating whole foods has proved to be anything but boring.

I wasn't born craving whole and real foods—most people I have met weren't either. For me, it's been an ever-evolving transformation. There was a period when I was devouring fast-food double bacon cheeseburgers and chocolate milkshakes and eating large bags of peanut butter M&M's as a snack. I was sneaking Pop-Tarts when no one was looking and feasting on greasy pepperoni pizza at two a.m. after a late night out. Then, swinging in the opposite direction, there was a time in my life when I counted my almonds as I ate them and was even afraid to eat a slice of focaccia while studying in Italy (who goes to Italy and is afraid of bread?!). I was petrified of cooking with any oil because of the fat content and didn't want to touch anything with a carb in it. I wouldn't even eat a cookie because I was so nervous I would gain weight.

We all have our ups and downs around food—a realization that felt so comforting once I understood it. We're not alone and we all struggle from time to time. It was during my struggles of putting weight back on and making peace with my body that I found a connection to the kitchen. My love for cooking and baking was born out of my rocky history with food and body image. I wanted to figure out how to fuel my body with food that was both nourishing and delicious. I knew that if I ate Reese's Peanut Butter Cups every day, I wouldn't feel good. But I wasn't about to give up dessert to feel healthy. Instead, I started making my own alternative recipes based on of whatever I was craving. Sure, my recipes are "healthy," but they are also easy and the results are delicious. My food looks and sounds a hundred times more indulgent than it really is, which is the best part! It's "food porn" that won't leave you in a coma or with a headache or a sugar high. Those Sea Salt Dark Chocolate Peanut Butter Bars on page 237?

They look like a super-gluttonous sugar bomb, but they're made of almond and coconut flour that's full of healthy fats and more nutrients than your typical white flour, and are sweetened with unrefined coconut sugar.

I want to inspire you and help you make a positive difference in your relationship with food. Being healthy doesn't mean saying no to the things you love or only drinking green juice or eating kale with every meal—that would be horribly boring. When you begin to fuel your body with nutrient-packed ingredients like avocado oil and sprouted spelt flour, you will notice a shift in how you feel—without missing out on all the good stuff. A nutritious meal can be delicious crispy quesadillas made with almond flour tortillas, pasture-raised eggs and nitrate-free bacon, and freshly made guacamole on the side. And you can for sure have a Homemade Dark Chocolate Caramel Candy Bar (page 246) for dessert afterward.

It has been a journey there and back, but I'm finally eating with no regrets and restrictions, and now I'm excited to share my stories and recipes with you to feed your body, your mind, and most important, your *soul* with quality food that tastes good and makes you feel good, too.

let's chat about how to use this book

As we continue to grow and learn more about ourselves, our tastes and cravings evolve. I ended up on the healthier end of the spectrum, and now I search out recipes that use real food and real ingredients. To me, eating "real food" means using ingredients you can pronounce (even the ones we struggle with, like quinoa), loading up on organic veggies, fruits, and raw nuts, and shying away from heavily processed ingredients, like hydrogenated oils and GMOs (genetically modified organisms). Yes, that includes healthy but comforting treats made without grain or dairy, like Layered Chocolate Chip Cookie Cake (page 254) and Spicy Cauliflower Wings (page 154). But that also includes occasionally eating cookies made with regular flour and sugar and enjoying a real bagel and lox when I'm craving it. (I hate to break it to you, but the birthday cake at parties isn't going anywhere. And your significant other will want to go out for pizza once in a while. Just because a couple of slices of pizza aren't going to give you a six-pack—which is overrated in my opinion, anyway—that doesn't mean they aren't good for your *soul* every so often!)

I favor unrefined sugars and alternative flours and oils, but I am definitely not down for sacrificing flavor. Food is meant to taste delicious. It should make you feel good. Food connects and brings us all together: whether it's dinner with friends, baking treats for your boyfriend or girlfriend, or getting that ice cream cone after a long-ass workweek, meals should excite us and warm our souls. But it shouldn't consume our minds 24/7 with thoughts of what will make us skinny and fit into those jeans we wore in college. These recipes will help free you from concerns that are unhealthy for both your mind and your body.

In this book, you'll find recipes for all your cravings—dishes that you want to eat, enjoy, and savor every bite of, including droolworthy desserts (see page 224), family-style recipes to bring to a potluck (see page 176), ideas for what to make when you're flying solo for dinner (see page 200), snacks to make for your besties and boo (see page 78), and more—recipes for pretty much all the parts of your life. You'll love these dishes whatever your cooking abilities. I am by no means a professional chef. I didn't go to culinary school. I'm not a registered dietitian or a health coach. I am just a twenty-something-year-old who loves to experiment in the kitchen and is like a kid in a candy store when I'm perusing the organic section at the grocery store. If I can make these dishes, I promise you can, too. My recipes won't take hours and hours of labor and don't require twenty-plus ingredients that you will never use again. There won't be a million confusing steps to get to the end (besides those Homemade Grain-Free Frosted Blueberry

Pastry Tarts on page 93—but they're *worth it*). I focus on whole foods—no crazy potions and fancy ingredients over here. To make it even easier, I show you what is in my pantry (on page 15) and how I food prep (on page 35) to help make the weekdays much less stressful.

I also want to give you more than just my go-to gluten-free chocolate chip cookie recipe (see page 242). I am sharing stories of my personal journey at the start of each chapter, dishing out all the details—from how I found peace with my body to that time when I didn't eat meat for five years. These include some of my most vulnerable stories, thoughts, and struggles because without these experiences, I wouldn't be where I am today. Sounds cheesy, right? But through cooking and finding the freedom to eat foods that make me feel good, I have been able to grow as a person. I want to put myself out there and share those moments because I want each of you to know you are not alone in this. No matter what the situation is, we all struggle and need some delicious fuel and support to get us through it.

a note about labels

Am I vegan, gluten-free, paleo, dairy-free, or on the ketogenic diet? Nope, none of the above, but I sure do love foods under each of those labels. I crave a good, fudgy brownie and a crispy veggie burger with some sliced avocado and almond milk cheese on top. But I also love adding real feta cheese to my salads and grilling up a grass-fed lamb burger. So what does that make me? What label do I fall under?

I am Rachel—that is my label. I like to think I live a label-less life and *finally* have food freedom after years of bouncing between diets that were unhealthy for both my body and my mind. I now have the freedom to eat what my body is craving. That freedom means many things to me: Freedom to choose to eat baked sweet potato fries over conventional fries cooked in GMO canola oil. Freedom to eat that slice of gluten-filled pizza topped with mozzarella if I want it. And freedom to use ingredients like almond and coconut flour in my desserts if I think it tastes better and fuels my body better than all-purpose flour. I am living my life away from food labels that describe my "life and eating style." Labels sound scary and too permanent. I have certainly dabbled in labels before (we will get to that soon) and have found that living your life based on what *you* are craving and what *your* body wants trumps any label out there.

Sure, you will see throughout the book that the recipes are indeed labeled if they have options to be gluten-free, dairy-free, and so on. But, if you're dairy-free and the recipe calls for regular cheese, use nut cheese! If a paleo-labeled recipe calls for grain-free tortillas but you're fine with regular gluten-free, use them! We are each our own person and are allowed to dabble in a bit of everything and eat what we crave. There are many people who do have allergies or intolerances and need to shy away from gluten or dairy or whatever the ingredient may be. I completely understand and want you to know which recipes are safe for you so you can eat without hesitation. So look for the labels, but let's just try not to let them overpower us.

p = paleo

v = vegan

gf = gluten-free

df = dairy-free

nf = nut-free

fp = food prep–friendly

what's in my pantry, fridge + kitchen

my "can't live without" list

My kitchen is filled with nutrient-dense, organic, quality ingredients. Don't get it twisted: we don't have a super-large kitchen with endless storage. (Who does when you live in an apartment?) We even had to turn a coat closet into a pantry to fit everything! But this has made me really prioritize what I keep around to cook with.

I love having whole food options within reach for cooking, baking, and of course my favorite part of the day—snacking and dessert. Sure, this means weekly trips to the grocery store to stay stocked up, but I know that by keeping these staples in my kitchen, I am setting myself up for success.

These pantry and fridge staples are the basis for what you need to make pretty much every recipe in this book. (Don't be intimidated by this chapter—we are all different and I hope you will customize these lists to fit your own life.) I highlight my go-to flours, oils, and even which fruits and veggies to buy organic when you are navigating the grocery store. You will see that my must-haves are friendly for any dietary needs or lifestyle. Use this as a guide when you are revamping your kitchen and cleaning out all the heavily processed foods (you won't miss that canola oil, I promise!). I'm not preaching that you must buy every item I list here in order to eat healthy, but I do suggest keeping a majority of these ingredients on hand so you can enjoy the most flavorful and delicious recipes from this book at any time. I also recommend buying organic whenever possible to truly maximize the benefits of eating whole foods.

pantry +
fridge staples

Raw nuts + seeds: There are jars and jars and jars of various nut butters, raw nuts, and seeds in my pantry and fridge. I look for nut butters with little to no added ingredients or excess sugars. A little sea salt and we are good to go. I love to use various types of nut butters like **almond butter, cashew butter,** and **peanut butter** for baking, smearing on toast, or just spooning straight from the jar.

For anyone who is nut-free, **sunflower seed butter** and **creamy tahini** are other great options to keep on hand. Depending on the brand of nut butter you buy, it will be stored either in the fridge or in the pantry.

I also keep a variety of raw nuts like **almonds, cashews,** and **Brazil nuts** (my fave nut to snack on!). I love how diverse their uses can be—for example, using cashews as a cream cheese-like filling (see page 250) and to make Herbed Cashew Cheese (page 187). Heck, you can even make flour or nut milk with almonds—they are so versatile! I store all of my raw nuts in glass jars to keep them more organized. Ideally, these live in the fridge to

maintain freshness, but since I go through them so quickly, I do keep them in the pantry most of the time.

Flax seeds and **chia seeds** aren't cheap, but I promise you will use them. Especially in this book, a little goes a long way. I usually combine flaxseed meal (ground flax seeds) with water to make a vegan egg substitute (see page 29). Flax seeds are high in healthy fats and fiber, and you can sprinkle them on everything. Chia seeds have great omega-3 fatty acids, fiber, and protein. When soaked in liquid, chia seeds have a thick, gel-like consistency, and I use them in a variety of recipes, including Creamy 5-Ingredient

Chia Seed Pudding (page 52) and Berry Chia Jam (page 234). I try to store all opened packages of seeds in the fridge to retain freshness. Garden of Life is a personal favorite brand. Their chia and flax seeds are a staple.

Grass-fed butter + ghee: I love baking and cooking with both grass-fed butter and ghee. But what is the difference between butter and ghee? Because it is lactose-free, ghee seems to be easier for some people to digest. It can be used anywhere you would normally use butter. Please look for "grass-fed" for both butter and ghee so it is of the highest quality. I share my method for making homemade ghee on page 30 (it is so simple!). Grass-fed butter can be stored in the freezer or fridge and ghee can be kept in the pantry.

Cooking + baking oils: There was a time when I was afraid of oils, but it turns out I was just using the wrong ones! You will notice that I use only coconut oil, avocado oil, and toasted sesame oil in this book. They are great options for many different situations. **Coconut oil** is easy to bake and cook with. It's great to use instead of butter to make a recipe plant-based and dairy-free. I use extra-virgin coconut oil from Garden of Life, but if you don't favor the taste of coconut, a refined coconut oil is a better option. If you have only solid coconut oil on hand and see a recipe that calls for liquid coconut oil, simply melt the solid coconut oil in the microwave to get it to liquid form and allow it to cool before using it. **Avocado oil**

is my favorite oil for cooking because of its high-heat properties and neutral flavor. I use it in many of my savory recipes, including those featuring vegetables and meat. **Toasted sesame oil** is great to have on hand to use in Asian-inspired recipes—the flavor it adds is unreal. All oils are stored in the pantry.

Sugars + sweeteners: There is not one recipe in this book that uses a refined sugar, like brown sugar or cane sugar, in the key ingredients. I try to limit my intake of processed and refined sugars. Sure, I'll eat a sugary cookie or piece of chocolate—I am only human! But in my own kitchen, I limit the amount of refined sugars in my food. I use **coconut sugar** in most of my recipes for a dry sugar option. It works very well in baked goods like cookies (Coconut Sugar–Dusted Snickerdoodles on page 245), cakes (Layered Chocolate Chip Cookie Cake, page 254), and those epic cinnamon rolls (see page 53). For liquid sweeteners, **pure maple syrup** and **manuka honey** are two of my favorite options for denser, moist treats like banana breads (see page 45) and no-bake desserts (Fig + Honey Cashew Cheesecake Bars, page 250). Heating manuka honey does lessen its health benefits, so I recommend using it in no-bake recipes only. Manuka honey is also a bit of a splurge item, but a little goes a long way. I recommend Wedderspoon's Manuka Honey. I also use **Medjool dates** in many of my dessert recipes, too. Dates are very sweet and contain a high amount of fiber. They also have a neutral flavor that isn't too overpowering. I store my opened maple syrup bottles and dates in the fridge, while manuka honey and coconut sugar are kept in the pantry.

Grain-based and grain-free flours: There are so many flour options these days, it can be overwhelming. To make your life (and my life) easier, I use only a few types throughout this book. For grain-free flours, I use **almond flour** (not almond meal) made from blanched almonds. Almond flour is nutritionally dense and higher in fiber and protein compared with most flours. You will notice it is much more filling than your traditional all-purpose flour. I also love using **coconut flour.** Coconut

flour is a bit tricky to use because it absorbs a lot of liquid. In recipes that call for coconut flour, you'll see almost double the amount of wet ingredients (like eggs and milk) than you would in a recipe that uses traditional all-purpose flour or other grain-free flours. It works differently than other grain-free flours and therefore is harder to replace with an alternative. As a very rough guideline, if you're looking to use coconut flour instead of almond flour in a recipe, you will need to cut the amount of almond flour called for by three-fourths and most likely add another egg and more liquid as well. If a recipe calls for 1 cup almond flour, use ¼ cup coconut flour instead and keep an eye on the consistency to see if more liquid or eggs are needed. (To achieve the authentic flavor of the recipe, I recommend shying away from this substitution whenever possible.) I keep my opened grain-free flours in the fridge to maintain freshness.

For grain-based flours, I love both **gluten-free oat flour** and **sprouted spelt flour.** They are very easy to use and can usually be subbed for each other with a 1:1 ratio. Oat flour is simply made from rolled oats, so you can make it at home if you prefer (see page 29), using gluten-free oats or sprouted oats (I prefer these two varieties over traditional oats because they are easier to digest). Spelt flour is not gluten-free. If you have celiac or a very severe gluten sensitivity, please don't use sprouted spelt flour! Use gluten-free oat flour instead. I store all grain-based flours in the pantry.

Thickening flours: I keep **tapioca flour** in my fridge at all times for baking and cooking. It has a neutral flavor and I use it for thickening, the way you'd use cornstarch. However, it can be less inflammatory than cornstarch for most people. Once the package is opened, store it in the fridge to preserve freshness. (If you're avoiding gluten, make sure to seek out gluten-free tapioca.)

Grains + grain-free alternatives: A few of my favorite grain-based products to keep on hand are **sprouted gluten-free rolled oats** (I prefer sprouted because they are easier to digest), **granola** (look for lower-sugar options, preferably without canola oil, refined sugars, or brown rice syrup), **sprouted bread, gluten-free pasta, quinoa, rice,** and **soba noodles.** Sprouted rolled oats can easily be made into oat flour (see page 29), oat milk (see page 48), or just a warm, nourishing bowl of oatmeal. I love keeping grains like soba noodles on hand to make a quick and easy noodle bowl, and gluten-free pastas for some comforting mac and cheese (see page 123), especially because the dried pastas have a long shelf life. I store my grains in the pantry, but I do like to keep opened granola in the fridge so it stays extra crunchy (totally optional).

For grain-free products, I keep **grain-free tortilla chips, tortillas,** and various **grain-free crackers** in the pantry. They are made with ingredients like cassava flour and/or almond flour and can easily be made into bread crumbs by processing them in a food processor to be used in recipes like Bacon + Beef Meatballs (page 143). It's a great way to use the last crumbs in the bag or when the crackers get a little stale (which happens quickly with grain-free crackers and chips). Crackers and chips are stored in the pantry. I also love keeping some **grain-free granolas;** they are more nut-based, with no oats.

Cacao + dark chocolate: First things first: don't trust anyone who says they don't like chocolate (. . . kidding, but not really). A few of my dessert recipes, like the Sweet Potato Almond Butter Brownies (page 238), call for cacao powder. **Cacao powder** is 100 percent cacao, meaning it is unsweetened. For all of my recipes that call for dark chocolate chips or chunks, I do not use any that contain palm oil or soy. If I am using a bar, I simply chop it up with a sharp knife. Hu's Paleo Dark Chocolate Bars and Baking Gems are staples for me, both for snacking and baking. You can use any of their unrefined organic coconut sugar-sweetened chocolate varieties in these recipes. If sugar in general isn't your thing, you can use 100 percent cacao chocolate bars or **cacao nibs,** which have zero added sugar. The result won't be as sweet, but it will be lower in sugar. Store the chocolate in the pantry, or if you prefer snacking on chocolate with more of a crunch, keep it in the fridge—or even the freezer, where I store mine for snacking! (If you are avoiding dairy, make sure to seek out dairy-free dark chocolate.)

Baking powder: Baking powder is a leavening agent and helps baked goods to rise a bit. Traditionally, it has cornstarch in it, making it not paleo for those who follow that lifestyle. I share my recipe for my own DIY Paleo Baking Powder on page 29.

Pumpkin puree + sweet potato puree + organic unsweetened applesauce: These three ingredients, which add sweetness and moisture to recipes, can be subbed for one another in pretty much any recipe. Look for **unsweetened applesauce, pumpkin puree,** and **sweet potato puree.** Some brands are sneaky and will add cane sugar, which is totally unnecessary in my opinion. The recipe will still work if you accidentally bought a variety with sugar, but I find it to be a waste of sugar! Store any opened purees and applesauce in the fridge.

Nondairy milks: I use a variety of **unsweetened nondairy milks** in my kitchen. I look for unsweetened milks because they don't have added sugars, and I look for store-bought varieties with minimal ingredients. You can absolutely make your own at home, too (see page 48 for my Homemade Oat + Seed Milk). I love almond milk, oat milk, coconut milk—anything works! I also use **full-fat canned coconut milk** in recipes that need a thicker, cream-like consistency. Don't try to replace full-fat coconut milk with other nondairy milks—the results will be too watery. When you open a can of coconut milk, you'll see a

thicker layer on top: in some recipes you'll scoop up the thicker layer and use it, while in others you'll mix the thick with the thin. Store all opened bottled milks in the fridge and opened canned coconut milk in the fridge.

Protein powders: I use both **plant-based protein powder** and **collagen peptides** for added protein. In case you are scratching your head wondering what collagen is, collagen is the most abundant protein that is already in our bodies. It is said to help strengthen our hair, skin, and nails. Personally, it has also been helpful for my digestion and has been an easy protein option for my body to process. I use collagen peptides sourced from grass-fed cows, and also marine collagen from wild-caught fish. Both are great options and I see benefits from both. I add collagen to recipes like my Creamy 5-Ingredient Chia Seed Pudding (page 52) or I just add it to my hot tea every day since it dissolves in hot beverages. Collagen does not thicken a recipe; it will dissolve once warmed.

Plant-based protein powder is another great option to use for baking or in smoothies. I look for protein powders with no added soy, refined sugar, gluten, or dairy and with the simplest ingredients. I prefer protein powders that don't have a chalky texture and actually add good flavor to the recipe. This is a great option for any of my plant-based readers who want to add extra protein to their diet. Protein powder can work like regular flour and it thickens and adds texture to a recipe. I store both protein powders and collagen powders in the pantry. Garden of Life makes delicious plant-based flavored and unflavored protein powder.

Apple cider vinegar: Fermented apple juice, a.k.a. **apple cider vinegar,** is the cure to all, my mother-in-law always says. (When we have a sore throat, she tells us to gargle it.) It is filled with good bacteria and enzymes. I also use it in my Peanut Butter Cinnamon Rolls (page 53) instead of yeast. Look for a raw, "cold-pressed" brand with icky sediment on the bottom—that's how you'll know it's a good one. Store it in the fridge once opened.

Pure vanilla extract: A staple in most of my baking recipes, this extract adds a sweet vanilla flavor to recipes and you just need a dash of it. Keep in the pantry.

Spices and herbs: My spice cabinet is overflowing at all times. My husband, Jord, gets nervous opening it because it's like Jenga: when you take one out, they all come tumbling down. **Cinnamon** is my favorite spice for baking. I also like adding **nutmeg** and **ginger** to some dessert recipes. For more savory seasonings, I love using **sea salt, garlic powder, paprika, black pepper, turmeric, cayenne, chili powder, red pepper flakes, dried thyme, dried oregano,** and **Italian seasoning.** These are my favorites, but your pantry will of course reflect the flavors you love.

Coconut aminos: An absolute staple in our fridge! **Coconut aminos** is a delicious sauce made from coconut sap. It is rich, salty, and slightly sweet in flavor. It tastes a bit like soy sauce or tamari but is completely soy- and gluten-free.

Organic vegetables: You'll find a rundown of specific vegetables to buy organic on page 25, but when in doubt, always buy organic! A few of my favorite veggies to keep on hand are zucchini, Brussels sprouts, sweet potatoes (Japanese sweet potatoes are my go-to!), sweet onions, leafy greens, garlic, shiitake

mushrooms, and spaghetti squash. I store all veggies in the fridge (even onions and sweet potatoes to preserve freshness). You can buy many organic veggies frozen, which are great whether you live alone or cook for a larger family. So you always have them on hand.

Organic fruits: I always stock up on my go-to organic apples, berries, and bananas. (Fun fact about me: I eat a banana and a big-ass apple every day.) I always have limes and lemons on hand for cooking. Fresh figs are also a favorite when they're in season. Keep all your fruit in the fridge so it doesn't spoil as quickly.

Animal protein: Our fridge and freezer are always stocked with quality animal protein. No, it is not cheap to eat higher-quality meat, so I'm not going to lie to you and say it is completely affordable. But when it comes to food, I prefer to invest in quality over anything else. Of course, please do what works best for you and your budget. Our meat collection at home takes up almost our entire freezer because I like to buy in bulk when I can (especially when meat is on sale) so we always have protein on hand. I always have **pasture-raised eggs** on hand for baking and cooking. Pasture-raised eggs are the highest- quality, best eggs you can find and they have bright, vibrant yolks. They come from hens that get to spend their days outside in pastures and not cooped up in small cages or barns like conventionally raised hens.

I also keep **organic chicken** (whole chickens, chicken breasts, thighs, and tenders) on hand—and whole chickens are my favorite (see page 129 for cooking instructions). Choose pasture-raised or free-range organic chicken that is certified humane and contains no antibiotics or hormones.

Grass-fed and **grass-finished beef, bison,** and **lamb** are my go-to red meats. **Organic antibiotic-free ground turkey** is one of my weekly staples that I use especially for food prep (see page 37). Look for organic and antibiotic-free.

When I can find **wild salmon** and **fresh wild lump crabmeat,** it is a treat! I love a good piece of fatty wild Alaskan salmon. Try to stay clear of farm-raised fish. Even organic and "health" food stores sell farm-raised fish—so sneaky!

Bone broth is a daily staple in my life. I love cooking with it and drinking it straight up. It is great for the gut and an easy way to add collagen to your diet. Shop for bone broth the same way you do meat: organic when possible, grass-fed, and no added hormones.

Dairy + nondairy alternatives: I do consume moderate amounts of dairy. I'm not a huge cheese gal (weird, I know), but I love **goat's-** and **sheep's-milk cheese** on my pizzas, salads, and eggs.

Coconut, cashew, and **almond yogurts** and **cheeses** are my favorite nondairy options. Look for organic options with little to no added sugar. Store all dairy and nondairy alternatives in the fridge.

what ingredients to buy organic

I am one of those nerds who loves going to the grocery store and stocking up on food for the week, but I know that shopping for groceries can be intimidating for some. It's confusing: which groceries need to be organic and which ones not? Organic food is not cheap and that is something I had to digest once I began fueling my body with quality, whole and mostly organic ingredients.

I always say that when in doubt, buy organic. All of the oils, flours, and sweeteners I cook and bake with are organic. For fruits and vegetables, I ask myself, "Am I eating the skin?" If the answer is yes, you likely should buy organic. I always stay clear of GMOs as well and try to source local if possible. Try to follow those guidelines with everything from fruit, veggies, animal proteins, to grains and chocolate.

The fruits and vegetables in the following list are the ones that have exhibited the most pesticide residue when they've been tested. (Gross—we do *not* want to eat pesticides!) The items you don't necessarily need to buy organic are the ones that are less likely to be contaminated with pesticide residues—you can save money and purchase the conventional version. I buy organic whenever possible, but I totally understand wanting to save money, so please do what works for you!

I like to say that if you eat the skin of the item, buy it organic. If it is something you peel, organic isn't always as necessary.

Always buy organic:

Potatoes (all varieties)	Celery
	Carrots
Leafy greens	Brussels sprouts
Apples	Tomatoes
Nectarines	Peppers
Peaches	Berries
Pears	Mushrooms
Cherries	Coffee
Grapes	Tea
Onions	

Items that are okay to buy conventional:

Banana	Mango
Avocado	Eggplant
Pineapple	Honeydew melon
Cantaloupe	Grapefruit
Sweet peas	Kiwi
Papaya	Watermelon
Asparagus	

kitchen tools

I started my food blog in our 450-square-foot apartment. Needless to say, we did not have room for many kitchen tools. Even today with all the recipe testing I do, I really try to keep the fancy gadgets to a minimum. I list a few of my favorite kitchen tools below, but if you are living in a small or shared space, not to worry! These tools won't take up much room, and you can choose the ones from this list you'll use the most often. All of these fit into my apartment kitchen, and I have gotten crafty with making room when needed. I even use my coat closet as a pantry (#priorities).

Quality knives: Do yourself, and your hand, a favor and invest in a few good-quality knives. You don't need to go crazy, but a **chef's knife** and a **paring knife** will be helpful for your cooking. Make sure to sharpen them every few months, because a dull knife is dangerous to use (counterintuitive, but it's true!).

Cutting board: How else will you chop up all the vegetables for food prep? Easy to store, and if you buy one that's dishwasher-safe, cleanup is that much easier.

Measuring cups: These may seem obvious, but **measuring cups** are so necessary when it comes to baking and cooking. How else could you measure exactly the right amount of flour or oil? I like to keep a couple of sets on hand for times when I'm prepping or cooking up a storm. (There are many days when I have the 1-cup measuring cup filled with sticky peanut butter but then want to use it later to measure out some flour.)

Mixing bowls: My **glass mixing bowl set** was one of the best wedding gifts I received. The set has about ten bowls in graduated sizes, all dishwasher-safe. They're great to use while you're cooking, and I even use them as serving dishes for pastas and salads.

Glass container set: *So* key for food prep and storing foods. I like to use **glass containers** and avoid plastic as much as possible. I buy sets that include various sizes so I can use them for everything. This is how I pack food to bring with me on the go, too.

Rubber spatulas: Mixing your banana bread and scraping the bowl for every bit of the batter isn't happening without a **rubber spatula.** Nothing fancy, but we do keep different sizes of spatulas around. You will want a mix of large, medium, and small ones.

Rimmed baking sheet: I didn't invest in a large **rimmed baking sheet** until last year. I felt like the silliest person in the world when I finally got one and saw how epic it is to fit all the sliced sweet potato fries on one tray instead of three. I love having a couple of large rimmed trays on hand for food prepping, roasting, and baking. (I combine different veggies on one tray, which helps with less cleanup, too.)

Cast-iron skillet: It's the heaviest tool in my kitchen, but the **cast-iron skillet** is an absolute staple. It's a game changer for cooking and baking and it is pretty affordable and easy to cook with. I have a 10-inch cast-iron skillet and it does the trick. Cast iron may sound intimidating, but once you start using it, you will be obsessed. You can cook basically anything with it: meat (Jord's Roasted Chicken on

page 129, hello), eggs, veggies, cookie skillets, and more. To wash it, use a cast-iron cleaning brush and rinse the skillet with water right after using (don't use soap or it will strip the seasoning).

8-inch square + round baking dishes: These are the only two baking dishes you will need for this book. All my cakes, brownies, bars, and more are made in these. I recommend greasing them with coconut oil, grass-fed butter, or ghee before using them, or lining them well with parchment paper.

9 × 5-inch loaf pan: Ah, the **9 × 5 loaf pan** (preferably glass as it is easier to care for and can be tossed in the dishwasher), the infamous holder of my banana breads. It is likely the most used pan in my kitchen since I bake some sort of banana bread every week.

Muffin pan: For making muffins, of course, but also for those amazing Chocolate Lava Cakes (page 233). I also keep a mini-muffin pan around—when used with mini liners, it makes the most adorable mini treats.

Parchment goods: **Muffin cup liners, parchment paper,** and **parchment bags** are what I try use instead of tin foil, plastic wrap, or waxed paper. Whether it's a baking sheet with roasted veggies or a loaf pan with banana bread, I line everything I can with parchment to prevent sticking and to allow for easy removal and quick cleanup.

the room and the budget, invest in a quality full-size food processor. My mom always jokes that she has the same one from her wedding registry! They are so handy to have around.

Blender: There are many **blenders** to choose from and some can be very expensive. However, you'll want to have a quality blender that can actually blend a frozen banana and your favorite smoothie ingredients. I use my blender to make homemade Oat + Seed Milk (page 48) and Mint Cacao Chip "Ice Cream" (page 262).

Electric hand mixer: Not mandatory, but **hand mixers** are very helpful when it comes to whisking together batters and making sure everything is evenly combined. Plus, they don't take up too much room and I use this instead of a stand mixer for all of my recipes.

Food processor: I use my **food processor** pretty much every single day. It's how I make oat flour, easily shred veggies like carrots for muffins, and prepare homemade pestos. It is ideal for a quick chopping job. There are many different sizes. I found a $20 one at HomeGoods a few years ago that's large enough for only two cups of food, but that does the trick for smaller recipes. If you have

Spiralizer: One of the first things I bought when I started cooking was a **spiralizer.** Before it was trendy, people thought I was crazy for making my zucchini into noodles. I became obsessed with making zoodles (zucchini noodles), then sweet potato noodles, butternut squash noodles—everything! You can even spiralize an apple if you wanted to. A spiralizer allows you to turn your favorite vegetable into a noodle form and has helped me sneak veggies into my daily eats.

cooking FAQ

I receive lots of questions from my blog followers, and here are the commonly asked ones. These are the little tips and tricks I have learned over the past few years, such how to make homemade oat flour, save half an avocado, create a chocolate drizzle, and more. These tips will help make your life easier in the kitchen and you'll learn some easy hacks, too.

How do I make and use vegan egg substitutes? (a.k.a. What is a flax egg?):

To make recipes egg-free or vegan, I use flax eggs or chia eggs instead of pasture-raised egg in the recipe.

Flax egg

1 tablespoon ground flaxseed meal +
3 tablespoons filtered water = 1 egg.

Stir together flaxseed meal and water in a small bowl and place in the fridge, uncovered, to set for about 15 minutes before using.

Chia egg

1 tablespoon ground chia seeds +
3 tablespoons filtered water = 1 egg.

Stir together the chia seed and water in a small bowl, cover, and place in the fridge to set for about 15 minutes.

How do I make my own oat flour?

Oat flour, made from sprouted rolled oats, can be subbed for regular all-purpose flour in most recipes: 1 cup sprouted rolled oats = 1 cup oat flour. Add the uncooked oats to a food processor or blender and pulse until the oats are broken up into a fine flour. I prefer to use sprouted oats (both gluten-containing or gluten-free work) as opposed to unsprouted/regular oats because sprouted oats are easier for most people to digest.

How do I make my own paleo baking powder?

I make an easy DIY baking powder by mixing ½ cup cream of tartar with ¼ cup baking soda. Mix in a small jar with a tight lid and store it in the pantry or cool, dry place. It will keep for a couple of months.

How do I make my own gluten- and grain-free bread crumbs?

Store-bought varieties are available, but making your own is so easy. Here's how:

Process your favorite cassava flour tortilla chips (or other grain-free/gluten-free chips or crackers) in a food processor to break them up into crumbs. You can also toast some gluten-free bread and process it in a food processor to break it up into crumbs.

How do I ripen green bananas faster for baking?

Preheat the oven to 300°F. Place your unpeeled bananas on a parchment-lined baking sheet. Bake in the oven for 15 to 30 minutes, until the peel turns dark brown. Now you are banana-bread-ready (see page 45)!

How do I save half an avocado for later?

Save the skin after cutting your desired amount, and leave the pit in. Cover the unused exposed avocado with the reserved skin, place it in a sealed storage container, and refrigerate. It will stay good for 1 to 2 days. Gently shave off the brown part when you go to eat the rest of it.

How do I make my own ghee?

Cut up 1 pound of grass-fed butter cubes and place them in a medium saucepan. Melt the butter over medium heat for 15 to 20 minutes, allowing the butter to foam, bubble, and foam again. The ghee will be bright gold with reddish-brown flecks of milk solids on the bottom of the pan. Remove the pan from the heat and allow the ghee to cool for about 5 minutes. Line a small strainer with two layers of cheesecloth and set it over a mason jar. Strain the ghee into the jar and discard the solids that remain in the strainer. Allow the ghee to cool completely in the jar before sealing it. Store in the pantry; no need to refrigerate. You will get about 1½ cups of ghee from 1 pound of butter.

How do I make a creamy nut butter or chocolate drizzle?

Add the desired amount of nut butter or chocolate to a microwave-safe bowl and add a dash of coconut oil (I like to use a square dish for ease of drizzling). Microwave in 15-second increments, stirring after each one, until completely melted. Store any leftovers, sealed, in the pantry. The drizzle will be good for about a week.

Can I swap different types of nut butters in recipes?

You will notice that many recipes in this book use creamy nut butters. I sometimes specify "almond butter" or "peanut butter" for a particular recipe. If the ingredient list has a specific nut butter listed, that means I believe the recipe tastes best with that one—though it's not the only option. You can sub any nut butter for another one or even use a seed-based butter like sunflower. If I call for almond butter and you only have cashew butter on hand, make it work! (I also recommend using creamy nut butters over chunky for most baking recipes.)

I'm dairy-free! How do I make substitutions?

There are a just a few recipes in this book that use grass-fed butter or sheep's- and goat's-milk cheese. These recipes are very easy to sub. You can use coconut oil, ghee, or vegan butter in place of the butter, and nut-based cheese where I call for dairy-based cheese.

The recipe will still turn out delicious! So even if something isn't marked "dairy-free" in the book, it can become 100 percent dairy-free if you make the swap.

I'm nut-free! How do I make substitutions?

There is a reason I am a bit "nuts." It's likely because I consume many nuts and nut-based products. I love cooking and baking with them. Almond flour adds a great protein and healthy fat boost to recipes. Plus, a peanut butter drizzle on top of pancakes will stabilize your blood sugar more than maple syrup.

If you have a nut allergy or cannot eat them, I gotchu. First of all, I am giving you a hug via this book because that is not an easy allergy to have. You can sub sunflower seed butter or creamy tahini for nut butters. For almond flour, use gluten-free oat flour or sprouted spelt flour instead. For nut milk, use coconut milk (not the canned full-fat kind—the thinner and more liquid-y beverage found in the same section as almond milk) or oat milk instead (see page 48).

What's the best way to reheat leftovers?

Add a light layer of avocado oil to a skillet and add your desired amount of leftovers. Warm them over medium heat for about 1 to 2 minutes, then cover and warm over low heat for 5 to 10 minutes. Slow and steady wins the race here. You can also use

a microwave if that is most convenient for you (especially those working in an office and bringing food).

How long do your recipes stay good for?

I live my life by the five-day rule—eat the dish within five days of making it. Store leftovers in the fridge—since these are all-natural ingredients with no preservatives, they can spoil quickly! For longer storage, freeze leftovers for up to three months.

How do I clean my cast-iron skillet?

I don't use soap or a sponge to clean my cast-iron skillet—sounds gross, I know, but your usual soap and sponge will damage the seasoning. Instead, use warm water and a scrub brush. After cleaning the skillet with water, dry it well, add a dash of oil, smear it over the skillet with a paper towel, and store.

How do I quickly thaw frozen meat?

Ah, the dreaded moment where you realize you forgot to thaw the meat for dinner. Take the meat (still in the package) and place it in a large bowl or pot. Set it in the sink and run hot water on the package to soften it. Soak the package in the hot water for 15 to 30 minutes, until thawed.

What ingredients do you try to avoid in products?

High-fructose corn syrup, brown rice syrup, agave, sucralose, Splenda, carrageenan, food dyes, hydrogenated or partially hydrogenated oils, refined palm oil, cottonseed oil, parabens, artificial flavors, aspartame, trans fat, Equal, soy lecithin, and soy-anything! I personally don't feel well after eating soy-based products like tofu, tempeh, or even edamame, but it is different for everyone. If you do tolerate soy well, go for non-GMO and organic because it can be heavily processed.

What chocolate should I bake with?

I like to bake with a couple of different chocolate options. I keep dark chocolate bars on hand at all times, as well as some dark chocolate chips. You can use chocolate bars and cut them up into chunks, chocolate chips, or anything you desire for all the recipes that call for chocolate or chocolate chips. Sub cacao nibs for a no-sugar-added version, but it won't be as sweet!

Can I substitute X for Y ingredient? (a.k.a. questions about substitutions)

There are some ingredients that are interchangeable and some that are not. When I create recipes, I intentionally use certain ingredients, so please note that the ingredients I list are the ones I recommend. But allergies exist, so please modify as you need. Nut butters (see page 30) and nut milks, for example, are so easy to swap. You can sub any nut milk in the recipes here (unless a recipe calls for "full-fat coconut milk," which refers to the thick coconut milk from a can). I recommend unsweetened nut milks when cooking and either unsweetened or sweetened for baking.

Baking is like chemistry, so subbing flours is a bit tricky. Each recipe here has been carefully tested, so switching out the flours (or any ingredients, for that matter) may affect the texture and flavor of the baked good. For any recipes where subs are okay, they're listed in the recipe Notes. A few key rules to know when subbing: Oat and sprouted spelt flour can be a 1:1 sub for each other. Almond flour can usually be subbed for oat or sprouted spelt as well, but typically you need to use a bit more than is listed. Coconut flour is a beast of its own: it requires double the amount of wet ingredients as it is one thirsty flour! For tapioca flour, arrowroot flour can be a 1:1 sub.

How many calories are in your recipes?

Ah, the most common question I get, besides substitutions, relates to calories and carbs and macros. I have been a calorie counter in the past and it did not work for me. My mind was brainwashed into thinking that staying under a certain calorie threshold was what I had to do every single day and it was the only way to be "healthy." I cut out foods and I missed out on *a lot* of good food during that time. Now, I don't count calories, macros, carbs, fat, or anything! It doesn't work for me, but I fully recognize that this may work for some and I applaud anyone who can do this without getting carried away. Once I began eating mostly whole and real foods, I lost track of calories and focused on quality over quantity.

Are your recipes labeled for certain dietary needs/restrictions?

Absolutely! I specify if each recipe is vegan, gluten-free, dairy-free, paleo, and/or nut-free. The majority of the recipes in the book are allergy-friendly no matter what, and you can definitely modify the recipe to work for you.

What foods do you pack with you when you're going to be out all day?

I am definitely fortunate to have access to my kitchen pretty much all day, so I rarely have to pack meals to go. However, there are some days when I spend the morning and afternoon in the city and do pack food. Here's an example of what I'd bring with me to stay satisfied until dinner:

Breakfast: The Original Overnight Oats (page 49) with some nut butter and fresh fruit on top in glassware of choice. I also love using an almost-empty nut butter jar (great way to repurpose!)

Morning Snack: Organic apple or banana with a handful of mixed nuts, some nut butter, or a snack bar

Lunch: Ginger-Scallion Turkey Burgers with Spicy Coconut Peanut Sauce (page 130) packed over a salad of leafy greens with soba noodles, avocado, and some tortilla chips or crackers on the side

Afternoon Snack: Slice of my Classic Dark Chocolate Chip Banana Bread (page 44)

food prep essentials

a guide to getting ahead and prepping all the eats

Food prep is a weekly activity in our kitchen. You may also know this as "meal prep" but my approach to preparing food for the week ahead is a bit different than making a few dishes and getting bored of eating them by Tuesday.

Sunday is usually food prep day in our home. Jordan and I make a list of foods we want for the week, head to the grocery store, stock up on all the items, and come home to prep it all. Sounds daunting and time-consuming, I know. You are probably already planning what restaurant to order takeout from instead of getting involved in this crazy enterprise. But just stay with me for a bit and hear me out on why I love my food prep.

1. It's a Huge Time-Saver

Food prep is a great way to invest your time. On one day you spend a few hours cooking, preparing, and cleaning up in the kitchen—and you are set for an entire work or school week. By food prepping, you will have food in the fridge waiting for you to heat and eat after a long day at work—and no heavy cleanup afterward. Plus, if you prep with a friend, your spouse, or another family member, it's a quality bonding activity for you two! Of course Jord and I would rather be outside when we're in the kitchen prepping veggies on a nice day, but we love that we get some uninterrupted time together and we know it pays off during the week (especially those never-ending days when next thing you know it's seven p.m., you are starving, and a bowl of cereal just isn't going to cut it). We put on a podcast or music and just do the dang thing. Now we're just patiently waiting for Ezra to help us out!

2. It's Budget-Friendly

Food prep also helps us stay on a budget. Going to the grocery store just once a week with a set amount of money to spend makes keeping to a budget so much easier. (I also always try to use what I have on hand first before buying anything new, too. For example, if I have some frozen grass-fed beef in the freezer, I will be using that instead of buying new meat at the store.) No matter how chaotic the coming week looks, you are setting yourself up for a week of enjoying meals prepared at home with ingredients you trust. It makes it easy to pack lunch for work or school, too, meaning less money spent on $15 salads from the café next to your office. You're not going to head out for dinner and spend $25+ on an entrée when you know you have delicious food ready to eat at home.

3. You'll Be Eating Better-Quality Food

You are probably wondering if we just hide in our apartment eating homemade meals instead of eating out. And the answer is *no*. We do eat out occasionally and there are days when I want to meet a friend for lunch or dinner, but I try to space those dates out to no more than a couple of times per week. Eating fewer meals out also means you can pay more attention to the foods you are putting in your body. Making dishes from scratch is empowering and allows you to know what ingredients are going into your food. No gross oils or GMO-filled goods can creep in. No, I don't obsess when I eat those ingredients at a restaurant, but in my own kitchen it is nice to have that sense of control over what goes into my food. (Even at the grocery store, when you go only once a week on food-prep day, there's less room for those impulse purchases when you're ravenous after work, eating a bag of dark chocolate pretzels on line at the store.) Personally, food prep gives me a sense of ease. It doesn't need to be stressful, intimidating, or crazy time-consuming.

How to Food Prep

As I walk you through my method of food prep, you'll begin to see why this is one of my favorite activities, and hopefully it will no longer seem so daunting. This isn't meant to feel like a chore or something you *have to do*. No one is forcing you to do this! It's a habit I have reaped the benefits from and love spreading the word about.

Take a look at page 16 for a description of my favorite pantry and fridge staples. By keeping these ingredients on hand, you set yourself up for success for the week.

My approach: I call this practice "food prep" instead of "meal prep" because I am not making specific complete dishes. Preparing different individual ingredients, like building blocks, as basic and simple as possible, allows for easy customization throughout the week. This approach also allows for more variety throughout the week, and thus less chance to get bored. Sure, some weeks we make recipe-based dishes like a specific chili, soup, or pasta. But for the most part, we like to pick a few items from each food category and prep those. Some nights, you'll crave tacos or pizza, while others you'll want a big bowl of random goods you have on hand. Stock up on go-to add-ins, like avocados, tortillas, dips, and spreads, to make things more exciting. We are all about satisfying those cravings!

My usual lineup looks like this:

1. **Two types of quality protein (such as grass-fed beef, wild salmon, and antibiotic-free chicken or turkey)**
   - You can make these as fancy or as simple as you like. We love to roast a whole chicken (page 129) or make some Bacon + Beef Meatballs (page 143), for example. You can prep ground meats into burgers or simply cook them in crumble form with spices like paprika, garlic, and black pepper. Nothing fancy. This is perfect to add on top of a bowl of gluten-free pasta, to stir into an omelet, or to stuff in one of those Epic 5-Minute Quesadillas (page 206).
   - For portable, on-the-go protein, prep some canned wild tuna or salmon with avocado oil–based mayo or hard-boiled pasture-raised eggs.
   - To my plant-based readers: if you enjoy tofu or tempeh, they also are great to prepare ahead of time.

2. **Three or four different vegetables (see page 148 for recipes)**
   - Roast veggies (the more the better) in a couple of large baking sheets lined with parchment paper (less cleanup). Japanese sweet potato fries (see page 166) and roasted Brussels sprouts (see page 170) are my two favorites, but look for what is in season, too. I always try to include some starchy veggies (like butternut squash) and something green like broccoli rabe.
   - I also love to spiralize some veggies like zucchini, butternut squash, or sweet potato ahead of time, leaving them raw until I cook them later in the week. The uncooked spiralized veggies stay well in noodle form for up to 1 week.
   - Keep raw greens like arugula, baby spinach, or butter lettuce on hand—an easy way to get extra greens in with zero prep!

3. **One or two grains (such as quinoa pasta, farro, and basmati rice)**
   - I do not fill up on eating just veggies and protein. I like to have carbs with my meal, whether from sweet potatoes, tortilla chips, crackers, gluten-free grains, or a mix of each. These are great to prep so you can bring a protein-packed pasta salad to lunch or make a DIY burrito bowl for dinner.

4. **Two or three breakfast and snack ideas**
   - Food prep doesn't only mean lunch and

dinner. Having a breakfast ready in the morning will ensure that you actually get some quality nutrition instead of sipping on coffee during your commute and calling it breakfast. Nothing needs to be fancy here. Make some Original Overnight Oats (page 49), Chia Seed Pudding (page 52), banana bread (page 45), or muffins (page 62) to keep on hand for the week. (P.S.: You can always cheat and buy ready-to-eat overnight oats.) There's also nothing wrong with making some cookies for the week, too. Post-dinner sweets are a staple in our home.

5. One or two dips or condiments

- I totally cheat sometimes (okay—very often) in the dip department. I love making my own Jalapeño Cashew Cheese (page 109) and Avocado Cream (page 140), but I do also buy condiments like Dijon mustard or almond milk chive cream cheese to use in various meals. These items make meals a hundred times tastier and more delicious!

In the Solo Meals chapter (page 200), I walk you through some of my favorite meals to make for one person. Most of the recipes are created from ingredients you prep ahead of time because it makes those meals even quicker to prepare. That way, when you're done with work, you don't need to start roasting carrots and broiling salmon—they're already ready to go!

Now let's walk through some of the most frequently asked questions I get about food prep:

Q: How long does the food last?
A: I like to live by the five-day rule: if I prep food on Sunday, I like to eat it all by Thursday or Friday that week. We rarely ever have leftovers since we prep the amount we need. There are some items that spoil quicker (like the Garlicky Kale Caesar Salad on page 157 and any type of scrambled egg dish); for those you'll want to stick to a day or two max.

Q: How much food do I prep?

A: The amount you prepare should be customized for *you*. It depends on how hungry you are and how many meals you want to get out of this food prep. Start off with less food in the beginning so you can test the waters.

Q: How long does it take to do this prep from start to finish?

A: I budget about three hours total, but this isn't *The Amazing Race*. If you make it fun, it doesn't need to be rushed. Cleanup can be minimal if you reuse the same skillets and pans. I also like to clean up at the end, so I clean only once.

Q: What do you store your prepped food in?

A: Usually glass storage containers, mason jars, anything I have on hand that has a tight seal. Even though the glass ones are much heavier to lug around, I do prefer to use them over plastic.

Q: Do you have a social life even though you food prep?

A: *Yes!* I try to aim for one or two dinners or lunches out per week. Of course, there are weeks with more or less eating out, depending on our schedules. Before prepping, try to have an idea of your plans for that upcoming week.

Grocery shopping: Am I the only one who gets giddy over a trip to the grocery store? I swear I can spend hours getting lost in the aisles, exploring and looking at new products to try. But I get that not everyone wants to allocate all their weekend time to a store. Here are my tips to make those trips as efficient as possible.

Tips

- **Make a list of what you need and are craving and stick to it!** Listening to your cravings is key: Shopping for what you think you *should* buy will likely lead to not wanting to eat it and the food going to waste. Buy whole foods that you crave and will fuel you.

- **Never grocery shop on an empty stomach.** I like to make sure I eat a meal beforehand or bring a snack with me while I shop in order to avoid unnecessary purhcases.

- **Grocery shop twice a week max to help keep food bills down.** Take stock of what you have at home (like that beef in the freezer) and use it up before getting anything new.

- **Become a crazy coupon person.** I am the one in line at the checkout holding everyone up with my coupons. Many brands will generously offer coupons if you haven't tried their products before, too. Also, many products have a coupon somewhere on the packaging, so look out for those (especially beverages, including kombucha). Stock up on items that are on sale.

- **Bring your own bags!** Invest in a few large totes that you can bring with you, and leave them in your car. I even bring produce bags!

- **Compare prices from store to store.** There can be a huge price difference on some items from one store to another.

sample weekly grocery list

Here is an example of what's on my list when I am stocking up for the week. Some weeks vary, based on inventory and what I already have on hand. Please refer to my pantry staples on page 16 for a full rundown on what I keep on hand at all times (flours, grains, oils, etc.). Your list will vary according to what you already have. Some weeks your list may be longer or shorter—it's all about what works for you.

Produce:

- ✓ Organic apples
- ✓ Bananas
- ✓ Organic sweet potatoes
- ✓ Organic berries
- ✓ Organic onions
- ✓ Lemons
- ✓ Organic Brussels sprouts
- ✓ Organic Swiss chard
- ✓ Avocados
- ✓ Organic leafy greens

Frozen goods:

- ✓ Frozen organic blueberries
- ✓ Frozen organic veggies
- ✓ Organic bone broth

Proteins:

- ✓ Free-range chicken (whole, breast, or thighs)
- ✓ Wild salmon
- ✓ Pasture-raised eggs

Specialty items:

- ✓ Grain-free tortillas
- ✓ Sprouted bread or bagels
- ✓ Dairy or nondairy cheese (I love getting sheep's- or goat's-milk feta)
- ✓ Nut butter
- ✓ Dairy-free dark chocolate
- ✓ Kimchi (look for vegetarian brands, if preferred)
- ✓ Snacks
- ✓ Nut-based or coconut-based yogurt
- ✓ Kombucha
- ✓ Sparkling waters
- ✓ Nondairy milk

breakfast

First Things First:
Sweet and Savory
Recipes to
Start the Day

It's crazy to think that my career started because of my love for overnight oats. I was born with a passion for breakfast food and all things oatmeal, granola, and peanut butter. My dad has been making oatmeal for as long as I can remember, and to this day the smell of rolled oats cooking is one of my favorite aromas in the whole world. I used to pack my overnight oats when I was fresh out of college. My coworkers would laugh and tell me I was eating "mush." But then they slowly started making overnight oats, too, and next thing you know, a whole office was eating them.

Fast forward to March 2015: I was sitting next to my now-husband, Jordan. We were doing pretty well financially, but we certainly weren't in a position to go out and spend $100-plus on dinner at a trendy new place. We were trying to get our feet on the ground while also making sure we had money for rent and for our future. There were so many things to do right outside our apartment door, but I wasn't making enough of a salary to experience all that was available. What kind of city life is that?

I told Jordan that I was going to start selling overnight oats in a jar, delivering them throughout the city. Like a side hustle of sorts, since I already had a full-time job.

(I had looked into walking dogs and babysitting, too—it was pretty much about extra income.) No business plan or strategy, just an idea and a brain running a million miles an hour.

Jordan was very supportive, but he recommended that I create a blog to see if there was any excitement around overnight oats before looking for a commercial kitchen to work in. As a blog reader for years, I had no confidence in starting my own. Me? Blog?

I never imagined anyone would be remotely interested in my recipes. But per Jordan's motivation, I started to post recipe ideas, ingredients I was into, and pretty much anything food- and wellness-related on my Instagram and then on my blog. Eventually I shared not only overnight oat recipes but muffins, cookies, and savory eats, too—all made in our 450-square-foot studio apartment.

I was shocked to see that people besides my family and friends were enjoying my recipes—how cool is that? I quickly abandoned the idea of selling overnight oats and focused purely on recipe development. I truly love creating recipes that both fuel our bodies and satisfy our taste buds, and breakfast food sure is my favorite food to prepare and to eat.

> Even if it is nine p.m., pancakes taste good to me!

Not in the mood for chocolate? I'll forgive ya! Sub fresh berries or your favorite chopped nuts.

classic dark chocolate chip
banana bread

 Of all things, it was banana bread that made my blog and Instagram take off. It went viral! To this day, banana breads are the most popular recipes on the blog (I have over ten kinds!). But let me tell you, I have made and eaten many banana breads in my lifetime and this recipe is the best. It combines all of my favorite banana bread recipes into one vegan, gluten-free loaf. There is something about the moistness (gross word, but such an accurate description) and richness of the melted chocolate chips and cooked bananas that lures me every time. Enjoy it with breakfast, as a snack, or for a sweet something after dinner.

v gf df fp

MAKES ONE 9 × 5-INCH LOAF

2 tablespoons **liquid coconut oil**, plus more for greasing the pan

1 **flax egg** (see page 29)

1½ cups mashed ripe **banana** (about 3 medium bananas)

½ cup **creamy seed or nut butter**

2 tablespoons **pure maple syrup**

⅔ cup plus 2 tablespoons **unsweetened nondairy milk**

1 teaspoon **pure vanilla extract**

2½ cups **gluten-free oat flour**

¼ cup sprouted **gluten-free rolled oats**

½ teaspoon **ground cinnamon**

1 teaspoon **DIY Paleo Baking Powder** (page 29)

½ cup chopped **dairy-free dark chocolate**

1. Preheat the oven to 350°F, and grease a 9 × 5-inch loaf pan with coconut oil or line it with parchment paper.

2. In a large bowl, mix together the flax egg, banana, seed butter, maple syrup, nondairy milk, vanilla, and coconut oil until well combined.

3. Add the oat flour, rolled oats, cinnamon, and baking powder and mix until well combined. Fold in the dark chocolate.

4. Pour the batter into the prepared loaf pan and smooth out the top with a spatula.

5. Bake for about 45 minutes, until the edges and top are lightly golden and a toothpick inserted into the center of the loaf comes out clean. Let the bread cool in the pan for about 30 minutes before removing it from the pan and slicing. Store in an airtight container for up to 5 days.

Don't have ripe bananas? See the tip on page 29.

paleo everything **bagel bread**

When I was in high school and college, bagels were considered a major food group. Of course I still love them today, but while they're delicious and good for the soul, they don't provide much nutritional value. This Paleo Everything Bagel Bread is a healthier twist on your typical bagel. It is made with an almond flour base and will fuel your morning more than any traditional bagel would—no more carb coma. Sure, a real bagel is 100 percent delicious and is toasted up in our home a couple of times a month, but who wants to have bagel-time only every once in a while? Add any toppings you'd like to this bread—my fave combo is smoked wild salmon, a nut-based cream "cheese" of sorts, and mashed avocado with fresh arugula on top.

MAKES ONE 9 × 5-INCH LOAF

1 tablespoon **avocado oil**, plus more for greasing the pan

2 cups blanched **almond flour**

¼ cup **flaxseed meal**

2 tablespoons **coconut flour**

4 teaspoons **DIY Paleo Baking Powder** (page 29)

5 large pasture-raised **eggs**

2 teaspoons **apple cider vinegar**

Everything Bagel Seasoning Blend

1 teaspoon **garlic powder**

2 teaspoons **sesame seeds**

2 teaspoons **poppy seeds**

½ teaspoon **sea salt**

1. Preheat the oven to 350°F and grease a 9 × 5-inch loaf pan with avocado oil.

2. In a food processor, pulse the almond flour, flaxseed meal, coconut flour, and baking powder until combined. (If you don't have a food processor, use a spatula to mix the ingredients together in a large bowl.)

3. Add the eggs, apple cider vinegar, and avocado oil, and pulse (or mix) until the dough is thoroughly combined and bit "spongy."

4. Transfer the dough to the prepared loaf pan and smooth out the top with a spatula. Sprinkle the garlic powder, sesame seeds, poppy seeds, and salt over the top.

5. Bake for 30 to 35 minutes, until a toothpick inserted into the center of the loaf comes out clean. Let the bread cool in the pan for about 15 minutes before slicing. Store in an airtight container for up to 5 days.

Make it nut-free: sub 1¾ cups oat flour or spelt flour for the almond flour.

Don't have all the seasonings for this? I recommend Everything But the Bagel seasoning blend; it works perfectly!

homemade **oat** + **seed milk**

Oat milk has officially taken over as queen of the nondairy milks. A year ago, we would have been scratching our heads wondering what "oat milk" even meant—*How can you make milk from oats?* I am still trying to explain to people how almond milk is made! This oat milk is my favorite nut-free milk to make at home. It is so creamy and the subtle flavor from the sprouted oats and flax seeds is just right. It isn't overpowering at all, and you can use it in your coffee and smoothies and for baking, cooking, anything you desire, including Creamy 5-Ingredient Chia Seed Pudding (page 52), The Original Overnight Oats (page 49), and to dip my cookies into, of course! Jord loves adding the milk to his coffee along with some grass-fed butter and collagen peptides.

MAKES ABOUT 5 CUPS

1 cup sprouted **gluten-free rolled oats**

¼ cup **flaxseed**

4 cups **filtered water**

½ teaspoon **ground cinnamon**

1. Combine the oats, flaxseed, and water in a blender and blend on high speed until well combined, 1 to 2 minutes. Add the cinnamon and blend just to incorporate.

2. Transfer the oat milk to a large resealable jar or a few smaller jars. Store in an airtight container in the fridge and enjoy within 5 days.

Why no cheesecloth or straining? You can use a strainer or cheesecloth if you want to strain the milk. It is optional and will remove the oat "pulp," but it isn't necessary.

the original **overnight oats**

As you read on page 43, my entire brand started with my love of overnight oats. This is a classic, no-frills breakfast recipe that's totally satisfying and versatile. These oats were my go-to when I commuted into an office every day—I'd eat them on the bus ride into the city. On Sundays, I'd prep enough overnight oats for each day that I would want them for breakfast and stored individual containers in the fridge. There it would be: breakfast ready at my fingertips in the morning! It is impossible to get bored with overnight oats—get creative by adding any mix-ins you crave, like your favorite fruits, coconut flakes, and/or granola. Just don't forget a dreamy manuka honey drizzle on top.

SERVES 1

½ cup sprouted **gluten-free rolled oats**

¾ cup **unsweetened nondairy milk**

1 tablespoon **chia seeds**

½ teaspoon **ground cinnamon**

Topping Ideas

Seed or nut butter

Fresh fruit (such as berries or sliced banana)

Unsweetened coconut flakes

Granola

Manuka honey (Wedderspoon's is my fave)

1. In a small mason jar or other resealable container, combine the oats, nondairy milk, chia seeds, and cinnamon.

2. Secure the lid and shake well to thoroughly combine. Refrigerate overnight, or for up to 5 days.

3. Before eating, add your desired toppings. The oats are delicious cold, or they can be warmed for a couple of minutes in the microwave if you prefer.

Want to make these extra flavorful and wholesome? Add a flavored protein powder or some manuka honey when you prep the oats.

The Original
Overnight Oats

Creamy 5-Ingredient
Chia Seed Pudding

creamy 5-ingredient
chia seed pudding

Want the easiest breakfast ever (besides overnight oats, that is)? This chia seed pudding is always on my weekly rotation of breakfast dishes and is one of the best to food prep (see page 38). It's so filling and satisfying, and it's basically a canvas for toppings. You can even add your favorite protein powder or collagen peptides for an extra nutritional boost—heck, you can put both in there if you're feeling crazy! Blending the pudding makes it extra creamy, and you don't need to wait for it to set overnight if you want to eat it immediately. Plus, you don't get chia seeds stuck in your teeth! Add some crunchy granola on top and you will be in breakfast heaven.

SERVES 1

1 cup **unsweetened nondairy milk**

3 tablespoons **chia seeds**

1 to 2 tablespoons **protein powder** (optional)

1 tablespoon **creamy nut butter**

½ teaspoon **ground cinnamon**

Topping Ideas

Granola

Fruit

Coconut flakes

Cacao nibs

Creamy nut butter

1. In a blender, blend the nondairy milk, chia seeds, protein powder if using, nut butter, and cinnamon on medium speed until the mixture is evenly combined and has a creamy texture, about 30 seconds.

2. Pour the pudding into a bowl and add any desired toppings, or store the pudding in an airtight container in the fridge for up to 5 days and add the toppings just before eating.

Don't have a blender? Totally okay! Mix the ingredients together in a mason jar or other small glass container, and then allow the pudding to set overnight before eating. It won't be as creamy, but the chia seeds will expand in the milk and turn it into a delicious pudding.

Not a fan of protein powder? You can sub collagen peptides.

peanut butter cinnamon rolls
with coconut glaze

Thoughts on a whole chapter dedicated to cinnamon rolls? They're a personal favorite of mine and I'll admit there's never going to be a healthy cinnamon roll that tastes better than the classic at Cinnabon, but these are pretty darn close. Instead of drowning them in refined sugar, I use a homemade coconut glaze sweetened with a little pure maple syrup. These are a great treat to serve at brunch or when you feel like having my mom over for breakfast—they're her favorite and I don't blame her!

MAKES 8 CINNAMON ROLLS

Rolls

6 tablespoons **liquid coconut oil**, plus more for greasing the baking dish

1 cup **unsweetened nondairy milk**

2 teaspoons **apple cider vinegar**

2 teaspoons **pure vanilla extract**

2¾ cups sprouted **gluten-free oat flour**, plus more for dusting

3 teaspoons **baking powder**

3 tablespoons **coconut sugar**

Filling

3 tablespoons **coconut sugar**

3 tablespoons **creamy or chunky peanut butter**

1½ teaspoons **ground cinnamon**

1 tablespoon **liquid coconut oil**, plus more for brushing the dough

1. Preheat the oven to 400°F, and grease an 8-inch square or round baking dish with coconut oil or line it with parchment paper.

2. **Make the dough:** In a small bowl or liquid measuring cup, whisk together the nondairy milk, apple cider vinegar, and vanilla. Set aside for 10 to 15 minutes.

3. In a large bowl, combine the oat flour and baking powder and mix well. Mix in the coconut sugar, coconut oil, and the nondairy milk mixture until well combined and a dough forms.

4. **Make the filling:** In a small bowl, combine the coconut sugar, peanut butter, cinnamon, and coconut oil and mix well.

5. Transfer the dough to a floured surface, sprinkle more flour on top, and knead it three to five times, until the dough comes together.

6. Using a rolling pin or a clean glass bottle, roll the dough out to make a large rectangle about ¼ inch thick.

7. Brush the dough with coconut oil and spread the filling evenly over the dough. Starting with a long side, gently roll the dough to form a log. Use a sharp knife to cut the log into 8 rolls, each 1 to 1½ inches thick.

recipe and ingredients continue

Coconut Glaze

½ cup **coconut cream**
(see Note)

1 tablespoon **pure
maple syrup**

8. Place the rolls, cut-side down, in the prepared baking dish and bake until they are fully cooked on top, 12 to 15 minutes; don't overcook them or they will be dry!

9. **While the cinnamon rolls bake, make the coconut glaze:** Melt the coconut cream and maple syrup together in a small saucepan over medium heat and stir until well combined.

10. Drizzle the glaze over the warm cinnamon rolls and enjoy. Store leftovers in an airtight container in the fridge for up to 5 days.

Wondering what coconut cream is? Refrigerate a can of full-fat coconut milk overnight and scoop out the thick topping when you open the can.

Not craving peanut butter? Any nut butter will work. Creamy cashew and almond are both delicious here.

sweet breakfast pizza
with an oatmeal crust

Pizza in the morning, pizza in the evening, pizza at suppertime—how many of you know that pizza bagel commercial I'm referring to? If you ask me, you definitely *can* eat pizza anytime, and this sweet "pizza" with its delicious oatmeal crust is the perfect evidence of that. Coconut yogurt works as the "sauce," and the seed butter, granola, and fresh fruit are the toppings—the possibilities of which are endless. This is a personal favorite to make when I have friends or family coming over for breakfast or brunch. It's always so fun to start the day with this sweet brekkie pizza.

SERVES 6

3 tablespoons **liquid coconut oil**, plus more for greasing the pan

1 **flax egg** (see page 29)

2 cups sprouted **gluten-free rolled oats**

¾ cup **gluten-free oat flour**

½ cup **pure maple syrup**

1 teaspoon **pure vanilla extract**

1 teaspoon **ground cinnamon**

1 cup **coconut yogurt**

½ cup **mixed berries**

¼ cup **gluten-free granola**

¼ cup **creamy seed butter**

1. Preheat the oven to 350°F and grease a 9-inch round baking dish with coconut oil.

2. Add the flax egg, oats, oat flour, coconut oil, maple syrup, vanilla, and cinnamon to a large bowl and mix until combined.

3. Pour the batter into the prepared baking dish and press down firmly with a spatula to compact the crust on the bottom of the dish.

4. Bake the oatmeal crust until it is golden, about 10 minutes.

5. Remove the baking dish from the oven and let the crust cool for about 30 minutes. Spread the coconut yogurt across the top. Sprinkle the berries and granola over the yogurt. Drizzle the seed butter over the top. Slice and serve or store in an airtight container in the fridge for up to 5 days.

fluffy **vegan pancakes**

Caaaaakes! My love affair with fluffy pancakes started at a young age. My mom used to make me the dreamiest, biggest whole-wheat banana pancake with lots of chocolate chips, and I'd ask for seconds 99.9 percent of the time. The pancake was so big, it could barely fit on the plate. These super-fluffy vegan pancakes aren't plate-size, but they're so simple and easy, you'll never turn to a pancake mix again. Don't forget to stir in different mix-ins to spice things up (*cough* *extra mashed bananas and dark chocolate chips* *cough*).

Have some breakfast guests? These fluffy pancakes are perfect for everyone! They're super allergy-friendly and easy to make, so you can enjoy your guests *and* serve up a delicious breakfast.

MAKES 8 TO 10 PANCAKES

1 cup **gluten-free oat flour**

1 tablespoon **baking powder**

1 cup **unsweetened nondairy milk**

2 tablespoons **coconut oil**, plus more for greasing the skillet

3 tablespoons **protein powder** (plant-based, if needed; I like Garden of Life)

1 teaspoon **pure vanilla extract**

Mix-In Ideas

Chopped dairy-free dark chocolate

Fresh blueberries

Mashed or sliced bananas

1. In a large bowl, combine the oat flour, baking powder, nondairy milk, coconut oil, protein powder, and vanilla. Mix until the ingredients are well combined and there are no lumps. Fold in any mix-ins (or leave plain!).

2. Heat a large skillet over medium heat and grease it with coconut oil.

3. Pour 2 to 3 tablespoons of batter per pancake into the skillet. Cook until bubbles form on the surface, about 3 minutes, then flip and cook on the other side until cooked through, about 3 minutes more.

4. Serve the pancakes warm, with your desired toppings.

Tired of oat flour?
Sub 1 cup sprouted spelt flour or 1¼ cups almond flour.

Don't have protein powder? Add 3 extra tablespoons of oat or spelt flour instead.

Making this for breakfast? Pair it with your favorite yogurt and fresh fruit for an easy breakfast. Or toss some granola into a mug and chug it on the way to work (kidding . . . but not really).

crunchy tahini chocolate
grain-free granola

You can find me shoving handfuls of granola into my face at all times of the day. I usually cheat and munch on store-bought granola (we're all human), but making this tahini version is so easy and it has such a unique flavor with the chocolate and nuts—and, surprise, no grains!—that it's worth the time. Tahini contributes a subtle flavor—it's an underrated ingredient that's great to keep on hand. This granola is a delicious addition to your yogurt bowl, sprinkled on top of pancakes, or just to snack on out of hand, whichever you prefer. You know I'm all about the last option.

MAKES ABOUT 5 CUPS

¼ cup creamy **tahini**

1 tablespoon **liquid coconut oil**

1 teaspoon **pure vanilla extract**

½ teaspoon **ground cinnamon**

1 cup **raw cashews**

1 cup **raw pecans**

1 cup **raw almonds**

¼ cup **flaxseed**

¾ cup **unsweetened coconut flakes**

⅓ cup chopped **dairy-free dark chocolate** (I use Hu Baking Gems)

Tahini isn't your thing? You can sub any creamy seed or nut butter you wish.

1. Preheat the oven to 300°F and line a baking sheet with parchment paper.

2. In a medium saucepan, combine the tahini, coconut oil, vanilla, and cinnamon and cook over low heat until melted and well combined. Set it aside.

3. Combine the cashews, pecans, and almonds in a food processor and pulse briefly a few times to break them up into smaller pieces (do not overblend!).

4. Transfer the nuts to a large bowl, and add the flaxseed and coconut flakes.

5. Pour the tahini mixture into the bowl and mix well—the dry ingredients should be evenly coated.

6. Transfer the granola to the prepared baking sheet and press it down firmly to form into a rectangle. Bake, shaking the baking sheet gently every 10 minutes (not too hard or the clusters will break) until the granola is golden brown, 35 to 40 minutes.

7. Let the granola cool completely, then add the chopped dark chocolate and break up any large clusters. Store in a large resealable container. The granola will keep in the fridge for up to 2 weeks or in the freezer for several months.

bakery-style
zucchini-carrot muffins

What is it about muffins that makes them so comforting? It's the fact that they are basically cupcakes without the frosting on top. Most of the muffins we see in bakeries are jumbo in size and loaded with excess sugar and creepy oils. These delicious muffins are definitely big and fluffy and have that crunchy muffin top, but they're lightly sweetened with coconut sugar and the zucchini and carrots make them extra nutritious. If you warm up the muffin and smear some nut butter on top, you will be in heaven. And I promise, no extra muffin top for you included. Headed to a brunch or to visit a friend? These muffins are perfect to make ahead and serve.

v gf df fp

MAKES 10 TO 12 MUFFINS

⅓ cup **liquid coconut oil**, plus more for greasing the muffin cups

½ cup shredded **zucchini**

1 **flax egg** (see page 29)

1½ cups **unsweetened applesauce**

¼ cup **unsweetened nondairy milk**

½ teaspoon **pure vanilla extract**

2 cups **gluten-free oat flour**

⅓ cup **coconut sugar**

4 teaspoons **baking powder**

½ teaspoon **ground cinnamon**

⅓ cup shredded **carrots**

⅓ cup chopped **raw nuts or seeds** (any type)

1. Preheat the oven to 350°F, and line a 12-cup muffin pan with paper liners or grease the cups well with coconut oil.

2. Extract the excess moisture from the zucchini by wrapping it in a large paper towel or clean kitchen towel and squeezing, discarding the liquid.

3. In a large bowl, combine the flax egg, applesauce, nondairy milk, vanilla, and coconut oil and mix well.

4. Add the oat flour, coconut sugar, baking powder, and cinnamon and mix until well combined. Fold in the zucchini, carrots, and nuts.

5. Pour the batter into the muffin cups, filling each one about three-quarters of the way.

6. Bake until a toothpick inserted into the center of a muffin comes out clean, 25 to 28 minutes.

7. Serve warm or at room temperature. Store leftovers in an airtight container for up to 5 days.

Prefer regular egg over flax? No problem! Sub 1 pasture-raised egg for 1 flax egg.

Want to sweeten these up a bit? Sub 1½ cups mashed banana for the applesauce, or add a few tablespoons of pure maple syrup.

maple bacon banana **nut loaf**

The bacon and sweet maple combination in this bread is unreal. Sure, there's the Classic Dark Chocolate Chip Banana Bread (page 45), but once you graduate from classic banana bread and make this Maple Bacon Banana Nut Loaf, that's when the real party happens. It is the perfect mix of a little salty and a little sweet. Any bacon lover in your life will go absolutely nuts over it!

Want to turn these into muffins? The batter will yield about 9 muffins. Bake until a toothpick inserted in the center of a muffin comes out clean, 10 to 12 minutes.

MAKES ONE 9 × 5-INCH LOAF

Coconut oil, for greasing the pan

1 cup mashed ripe **banana** (about 2 medium bananas)

½ cup **creamy nut butter**

¼ cup **pure maple syrup**

3 large pasture-raised **eggs**

1 teaspoon **pure vanilla extract**

½ cup **coconut flour**

2 teaspoons **DIY Paleo Baking Powder** (page 29)

1 teaspoon **ground cinnamon**

⅓ cup chopped, cooked nitrate-free, sugar-free **bacon**

2 tablespoons **coconut sugar**

⅓ cup coarsely chopped **raw nuts** (such as pecans or walnuts)

1. Preheat the oven to 350°F, and grease a 9 × 5-inch loaf pan with coconut oil or line it with parchment paper.

2. In a large bowl, combine the banana, nut butter, maple syrup, eggs, and vanilla and mix well. Add the coconut flour, baking powder, and ½ teaspoon of the cinnamon and mix again until the batter is well combined. Fold in the bacon and pour the batter into the prepared loaf pan.

3. In a small bowl, mix the remaining ½ teaspoon cinnamon with the coconut sugar.

4. Sprinkle the chopped nuts and cinnamon sugar over the batter.

5. Bake until a toothpick inserted into the center of the loaf comes out clean, 35 to 45 minutes.

6. Allow the loaf to cool in the pan for 20 to 30 minutes before serving. Any leftover bread will keep in the freezer for up to 2 months.

Don't eat bacon? Sub coconut bacon (see page 150) or your favorite mix-in, such as dark chocolate chips or fresh blueberries.

Don't have ripe bananas ready? See the tip on page 29.

Nut-free? Omit the crushed nuts and add chocolate chips or seeds instead.

dreamy coconut flour
breakfast cake

We are combining two of life's greatest eats into one recipe here: think cake meets pancakes meets straight-up heaven. This breakfast cake, a healthier version of a Dutch pancake, is made with coconut flour, so it's filling, satisfying, and flavorful. Enjoy the cake for breakfast over the course of a few days or share it with friends for a brunch at home. It tastes sweet enough to even be enjoyed as dessert. Try topping the cake with some fresh berries, coconut yogurt, and a drizzle of nut butter. You won't regret it.

SERVES 4

Coconut oil, for greasing the pan

½ cup coconut flour

4 teaspoons DIY Paleo Baking Powder (page 29)

1 teaspoon ground cinnamon

⅓ cup mashed ripe banana (about 1 medium banana)

2 teaspoons pure vanilla extract

7 tablespoons unsweetened nondairy milk

4 large pasture-raised eggs

2 tablespoons pure maple syrup (optional)

Mix-In Ideas

Berries

Sliced banana

Dairy-free dark chocolate chunks

1. Preheat the oven to 350°F and grease an 8-inch ovenproof skillet with coconut oil.

2. In a large bowl, mix together the coconut flour, baking powder, and cinnamon.

3. In a separate large bowl, mix together the mashed banana, vanilla, and nondairy milk. Beat in the eggs one at a time until well combined. Add the maple syrup, if using.

4. Pour the wet ingredients into the dry ingredients and stir until well combined and smooth (do not overmix). Let the batter sit until it has thickened, about 5 minutes.

5. Fold in any desired mix-ins and pour the batter into the greased skillet.

6. Bake until the top and sides are golden brown, 25 to 30 minutes.

7. Enjoy immediately or store in the fridge. The cake will keep in the fridge for up to 5 days. Reheat it in a 350°F oven for 5 to 10 minutes before serving.

carrot cake smoothie bowl
with cinnamon crunchies

We all love a good homemade smoothie bowl, and I don't know about you, but half the time I don't even follow a recipe. Throwing a bunch of ingredients you have on hand into a blender and then topping the smoothie with whatever you want is definitely liberating! But when I made this epic breakfast bowl that tasted like I was eating carrot cake with Cinnamon Toast Crunch on top, I knew it was a keeper. Plus, veggies for breakfast? Ya baby, you get extra points for that today.

SERVES 1

Cinnamon Crunchies

1 teaspoon **liquid coconut oil**

2 tablespoons **unsweetened coconut flakes**

2 tablespoons chopped **raw nuts** (any type)

½ teaspoon **ground cinnamon**

Smoothie Bowl

1 medium frozen **banana**

⅓ cup chopped frozen **carrots**

1 tablespoon **creamy nut butter**

2 tablespoons vanilla plant-based **protein powder**

½ teaspoon **ground cinnamon**

¼ teaspoon **ground nutmeg**

⅓ cup **unsweetened nondairy milk**

Topping Ideas

Granola

Raw walnuts

1. **Make the cinnamon crunchies:** Heat the coconut oil in a small skillet set over medium heat and add the coconut flakes, chopped nuts, and cinnamon. Toast, stirring frequently, until fragrant, 3 to 5 minutes. Remove the skillet from the heat and set it aside.

2. **Make the smoothie bowl:** Blend the banana, carrots, nut butter, protein powder, cinnamon, nutmeg, and nondairy milk in a blender on medium-high speed until creamy.

3. Pour the smoothie into a bowl and top it with the cinnamon crunchies and any other desired toppings. Enjoy it cold.

Making the smoothie ahead of time? Store it in the freezer overnight, and store the cinnamon crunchies separately in the fridge. The next morning, let the smoothie bowl thaw for about 10 to 15 minutes on the counter. Top it with the crunchies and dig in.

chocolate chip
sweet potato waffles

What is a cookbook without some crazy good waffles in it? Both waffles and pancakes (see page 58) are staples in our home no matter what day of the week it is. Weekend mornings, you can find me making a fresh batch of waffles so we can enjoy them later in the week for breakfast or snacking. These waffles, made with sweet potato puree and almond flour, are simple and satisfying. The sweet potato makes these waffles amazing for their flavor and color, and of course we love getting those veggies at breakfast again!

MAKES 4 OR 5 WAFFLES

1 tablespoon **liquid coconut oil**, plus more for greasing the waffle iron

½ cup **sweet potato puree** (see page 238)

2 large pasture-raised **eggs**

⅓ cup **unsweetened nondairy milk**

1 teaspoon **pure vanilla extract**

1 cup blanched **almond flour**

2 tablespoons **coconut flour**

1 teaspoon **DIY Paleo Baking Powder** (page 29)

1 teaspoon **ground cinnamon**

⅓ cup chopped **dairy-free dark chocolate**

Pure maple syrup or **creamy nut butter**, for serving

1. Preheat a waffle iron according to the manufacturer's instructions and grease it well with coconut oil.

2. In a large bowl, combine the coconut oil, sweet potato, eggs, nondairy milk, and vanilla. Mix well.

3. Add the almond flour, coconut flour, baking powder, and cinnamon and mix again until well combined. Fold in the dark chocolate.

4. Add 2 to 3 spoonfuls of batter per waffle to the heated waffle iron. Cook according to the waffle iron instructions, until fluffy. Do not undercook or the waffles will fall apart.

5. Enjoy the waffles with maple syrup or a creamy nut butter drizzle. Extra waffles will keep in an airtight container in the freezer for up to 2 months. Thaw and toast them or crisp them in a skillet before serving.

Don't like sweet potatoes? Sub ½ cup pumpkin puree or ½ cup mashed banana for the sweet potato.

To make it nut-free: sub ¾ cup oat flour or sprouted spelt flour for the almond flour.

baked peanut butter + jelly
french toast

Compared to pancakes and waffles, French toast is often the forgotten child in the breakfast world. But in our home, I always dream of that thick challah French toast my mom used to make—drowning in maple syrup with extra cinnamon, please. When you typically think of French toast, you're likely imagining it crisped in a large skillet on the stove. But not this recipe! Made in the oven instead, it still gets extra crispy, no pan-frying needed. Plus, it has the dreamiest flavor combo thanks to the peanut butter and berries. Such an easy recipe with minimal cleanup!

SERVES 5

Liquid **coconut oil**, for greasing the pan

3 large pasture-raised **eggs**

¾ cup **unsweetened nondairy milk**

1½ tablespoons **pure maple syrup**, plus more for serving

½ teaspoon **ground cinnamon**

½ teaspoon **pure vanilla extract**

10 slices **gluten-free bread**

¼ cup creamy **peanut butter**

½ cup frozen **blueberries**, chopped **strawberries**, or **raspberries**, thawed (see Note)

1. Preheat the oven to 350°F. Line a baking sheet with parchment paper and grease the paper with coconut oil.

2. In a large bowl, whisk together the eggs, nondairy milk, maple syrup, cinnamon, and vanilla.

3. Dip a slice of bread into the batter, letting the excess drip back into the bowl, and place it on the prepared baking sheet. Repeat with the remaining slices. Smear each slice with peanut butter and top with the berries, mashing them a bit with a fork.

4. Bake until the batter has soaked in and the bread is golden brown, 25 to 30 minutes.

5. Top the French toast with maple syrup and serve it warm. Store any leftovers in an airtight container in the fridge for up to 5 days. Reheat them in a cast-iron skillet that has been greased with a bit of coconut oil or grass-fed butter.

Don't have frozen berries? Fresh berries can work as well, but frozen usually have a better texture for this.

Don't eat eggs? Sub 3 flax eggs (see page 29) for the 3 pasture-raised eggs.

breakfast

mushroom quiche
with zucchini hash-brown crust

Ah, savory breakfast, we finally meet. Are any of you also guilty of eating sweet things for breakfast pretty much seven days a week? I'm usually more into eating eggs for lunch or dinner, but there are mornings when eggs sound just perfect. Eggs are a versatile, easy, and affordable protein option. This quiche has a zucchini hash-brown crust and is perfect to prep and then eat throughout the week. You can switch up the veggies in the filling, and feel free to add some nitrate-free bacon or sausage for all those meat lovers out there.

SERVES 4

Avocado oil, for greasing the baking dish

1 cup shredded **zucchini**

¼ cup diced **onion**

¼ cup blanched **almond flour**

6 large pasture-raised **eggs**

1 cup sliced **mushrooms**

½ teaspoon **garlic powder**

½ teaspoon **freshly ground black pepper**

¼ cup **unsweetened nondairy milk**

1. Preheat the oven to 350°F and grease an 8-inch round baking dish with avocado oil.

2. Extract the excess moisture from the zucchini by wrapping it in a large paper towel or clean kitchen towel and squeezing, discarding the liquid. Combine the zucchini with the onion and the almond flour in a medium bowl.

3. Add the zucchini-onion mixture to the prepared baking dish and press it down to form a flat crust.

4. Bake the crust so it begins to cook and crisp a bit, about 8 minutes (don't skip this step or the crust will be soggy).

5. In a medium bowl, whisk the eggs. Stir in the mushrooms, garlic powder, pepper, and nondairy milk.

6. Pour the filling over the crust and bake until the eggs are fully cooked and not jiggly, 15 to 18 minutes. Serve warm. Store any leftovers in an airtight container in the fridge for up to 5 days.

Want to make this more portable? Turn the quiche into egg muffins: Press the zucchini mixture into 9 cups of a greased 12-cup muffin pan and bake for 6 to 8 minutes. Pour in the egg filling and bake for 10 to 15 minutes more.

Not into almond flour? Sub ¼ cup gluten-free oat flour.

Want to make the cookies a bit sweeter? Add a few tablespoons of honey or maple syrup.

Don't eat eggs? Sub 2 flax eggs (see page 29) for the 2 pasture-raised eggs.

chunky oatmeal breakfast
collagen cookies

Ya, Ma, we are eating cookies for breakfast these days. These cookies are fully loaded with all the breakfast items we love, like sprouted rolled oats and nut butter. The added collagen peptides give you an extra nutritional boost and protein to start the morning. You can of course eat these cookies any time of the day, and it's perfectly acceptable to crumble them into your yogurt with some fresh berries and more nut butter drizzled on top.

Want to add something extra? Mix some fresh berries into the cookies before baking them. Blueberries and sliced blackberries are amazing in these cookies!

MAKES ABOUT 12 COOKIES

¾ cup blanched **almond flour**

¾ cup sprouted **gluten-free rolled oats**

¼ cup **unsweetened shredded coconut**

2 tablespoons **collagen peptides**

1 teaspoon **baking powder**

1 teaspoon **ground cinnamon**

2 pasture-raised **eggs**

½ cup **creamy nut butter**

3 tablespoons **liquid coconut oil**

1 teaspoon **pure vanilla extract**

¼ cup **cacao nibs**

Flaky **sea salt**, for sprinkling (optional)

1. Preheat the oven to 375°F and line a baking sheet with parchment paper.

2. In a large bowl, mix together the almond flour, oats, shredded coconut, collagen peptides, baking powder, and cinnamon.

3. In a medium bowl, mix together the eggs, nut butter, coconut oil, and vanilla until smooth and creamy.

4. Pour the wet ingredients into the dry ingredients and mix well. Fold in the cacao nibs.

5. Scoop 1 to 2 tablespoons of the dough into your hand and roll it to form a ball. (The mixture will be a bit dry and crumbly, but that's okay; if the dough isn't holding together, add a bit more nut butter.) Put them on the prepared baking sheet, lightly press each ball to flatten a bit, and sprinkle some salt on top, if desired.

6. Bake until lightly browned, about 10 minutes. Let the cookies cool on the baking sheet before serving. The cookies will keep in an airtight container at room temperature for up to 1 week, or frozen for up to 2 months.

snacks

Netflix and Chill:
Snacks to Whip Up
to Impress Your
Besties or Boo

So you have a new boo, huh? Or maybe a new friend you want to impress? Or perhaps you are just really in the mood to make some epic snacks for yourself. Any and all of the above work for this chapter, which is all about my favorite part of the day: *snackin'*. I can't go a day without snacking in some capacity (usually a few times, if I'm being honest). There is no shame in the snack game, my friends. But you know who is the real MVP of snacking? My husband and best friend, Jordan.

Jordan (a.k.a. Jord, J, or Jordie) and I met in college when I was nineteen. He was a year ahead of me and we would see each other everywhere: the dining hall, the gym, walking to class, at parties, you name it. Our paths would cross frequently and we would just make that awkward eye contact and not say hi.

I always wondered who he was, that guy wearing salmon-colored pants and bold glasses. A few weeks later, I bumped into him at a mutual friend's party and I mouthed my very first words to him: "Is there more beer in the fridge?" (I kid you not, that was the first thing I ever said to Jord.) We ended up making small talk, and when I went back to my dorm room later that night, despite my friends telling me "Don't do it!," I Facebook friended him. We met up again at a college event a couple weeks later and have been pretty much inseparable ever since. I was not interested in finding a boyfriend or being in a relationship at the time, but there was something about J. Call me crazy, but two weeks in, I knew I was going to marry him. His kindness and generous heart were something I had only dreamed of finding one day.

Jord and I were engaged at twenty-three, married at twenty-five, and I am truly the luckiest to have him by my side every single day. And now he's my baby daddy! Needless to say, lots of snacking happens now, especially while raising our little dude. Whether you're binge-watching your fave show or burning some palo santo, get snackin' on your favorite recipes, friends!

> Whether you're binge-watching your fave show or burning some palo santo, get snackin'

The Dreamiest
Apple Nachos

Nut Butter Banana Sushi

Sweet Toast

go-to snack combos

Hungry and looking for a snack to eat immediately? Story of my life. From a self-proclaimed professional snacker, here is a list of quick, easy, and always satisfying snacks. Most of these can be whipped up with ingredients you have on hand (now that your pantry is stocked with the goods—see page 16) and are super easy to bring to work or school, too.

Nut Butter Banana Sushi

Smear a large banana all over with nut butter. (My choices: creamy cashew butter or peanut butter.) Roll the covered banana in your choice of granola, coconut flakes, or anything crunchy, even cacao nibs. Slice it into ½-inch-thick pieces and enjoy.

The Dreamiest Apple Nachos

Core and slice an apple into 8 to 10 wedges. Drizzle some manuka honey on top of each piece and add any additional extra toppings (I usually go for some Grain-Free Granola [page 61] for crunch). Place a couple of tablespoons of nut butter in a small bowl. Dip the apple slices in the nut butter and enjoy!

Sweet Caramelized Banana Split

Warm a bit of coconut oil or ghee (see page 30) in a medium skillet over medium heat.

Slice a banana in half lengthwise and add the halves to the skillet, cut-side down. Sprinkle lots of cinnamon on top and cook until the banana is caramelized to your liking, about 5 minutes.

Transfer the banana to a plate and top it with some creamy nut butter so it gets all melty and delicious. Enjoy while it's still warm.

5-Minute Yogurt Snack Bowl

Spoon some of your favorite yogurt into a small bowl and top it with berries or other fresh fruit (I love blueberries or fresh figs), granola (a mix of grain and grain-free is delicious), some cacao nibs, flaxseed, and your drizzle of choice (honey, nut butter, and chocolate are all great). You can also add a mini muffin (see page 258) or a slice of banana bread in the bowl (see page 45).

Sweet or Savory Toast (see page 222)

Smear a slice of toast with mashed avocado and some red pepper flakes. Or, for something sweet, spread on some nut butter, mash fresh berries on top, and add a sprinkle of chia seeds. Look for sprouted bread—it is wholesome and easy to digest.

Smashed Avocado + Crackers or Chips

In a small bowl, mash some avocado (I use ⅓ to ½ avocado per serving). Season it, if desired, with a bit of black pepper, garlic powder, and sea salt. Add some fresh cilantro if you have it on hand. Scoop up the avocado mash with crackers or chips of your choice.

Granola-Stuffed Baked Apple

Preheat the oven to 375°F. Slice off the top of an apple and hollow out just the core with a spoon (leave the bottom intact). Spoon ⅓ cup granola into the cavity and bake until the apple is slightly softened, about 15 minutes. Top it with nut butter and unsweetened coconut flakes.

Crunchy Bowl with Nut Milk and Protein

Add your favorite granola or cereal to a bowl, pour your desired amount of milk on top, and mix in your favorite plant-based protein powder. The protein is optional but will make the snack more filling than the usual milk and granola.

Avocado + Smoked Wild Salmon on Rice Crackers

Mash half an avocado and spread it on about 4 rice crackers (depending on how big they are and how hungry you are). Top each cracker with a thin slice of smoked salmon. Sprinkle some sesame seeds or some Everything Bagel seasoning blend (see page 46) on top.

Snack Bar of Choice

I am definitely a snack bar gal. They are one of my favorite ways to get nutrients to give my body some fuel fast. There are *many* bars on the market, but I have narrowed the choice down to a few that I love and that satisfy my hunger. I always take these along when I'm traveling and keep them in my bag when I am out for the day.

nutty collagen **snackin' fudge**

Collagen is an absolute staple in my pantry (see page 21). Collagen peptides or marine collagen (from fish) can be used in a variety of recipes for an added nutritional boost. Collagen has made a difference in my hair, skin, and nails and it even helps with digestion and joint health! I use unflavored collagen peptides so you don't even know they're in there. This nutty fudge is completely sugar-free (no maple syrup or anything), packed with healthy fats and protein, and will satisfy your craving for something rich and indulgent.

MAKES 12 PIECES

2 cups **creamy cashew butter**

1½ cups blanched **almond flour**

3 tablespoons **cacao powder**

¼ cup **collagen peptides**

¼ cup **unsweetened nondairy milk**

⅓ cup **unsweetened coconut flakes**

⅓ cup chopped **raw nuts** (any type)

1. Line a 12-cup muffin pan with paper liners.

2. Add the cashew butter, almond flour, cacao powder, collagen peptides, and nondairy milk to a food processor. Pulse until the mixture is well combined and a dough is starting to form, scraping down the sides of the bowl as needed, about 2 minutes. Add the coconut flakes and chopped nuts and pulse a few times to incorporate.

3. Using a spoon, scoop the dough into the prepared muffin cups about three-fourths way full and press down to flatten it a bit.

4. Freeze for about 1 hour, until set. The cups will keep in an airtight container in the freezer for up to 2 months. No need to thaw the fudge before eating.

Nut-free? Sub ½ cup coconut flour for the almond flour and omit the chopped nuts (chocolate chips or cacao nibs would make a delicious addition).

almond flour "cheese" crackers

Anyone else grow up hating real cheese but loving Cheez-Its, Goldfish, and any artificial cheese snack? No? Just me? Okay, great. I used to snack on those salty crackers any chance I had. Of course they didn't actually taste like a piece of cheese, which is likely why I loved them so much. These cheese crackers, made with almond flour and nutritional yeast, are the modern-day version of those childhood favorites. As soon as you pop one in your mouth, you will feel as though you are back in fifth grade having your afternoon snack. They are delicious on their own or you can add them to a bowl of soup or dunk them into a favorite dip (the Herbed Cashew Cheese on page 187 is a match made in heaven).

MAKES ABOUT 60 CRACKERS

1 cup blanched **almond flour**, plus more for dusting

½ teaspoon **sea salt**

½ teaspoon **garlic powder**

2 tablespoons **nutritional yeast**

3 tablespoons **gluten-free tapioca flour**

3 tablespoons **avocado oil**, plus more for brushing

> **Don't eat almonds?** Sub 1 cup oat flour or sprouted spelt flour.

1. Preheat the oven to 350°F and line a baking sheet with parchment paper.

2. In a food processor, combine the almond flour, salt, garlic powder, nutritional yeast, and tapioca flour and pulse until combined.

3. Add the avocado oil and pulse a few times until the dough is crumbly. Add water, 1 tablespoon at a time, blending until the dough comes together in a ball (will be about 3 tablespoons of water total).

4. Divide the dough in half. Roll out each portion on a lightly floured surface to make a large rectangle about ⅛ inch thick. Slice the dough into 1-inch squares. Transfer the squares to the prepared baking sheet, spacing them about ½ inch apart.

5. Bake until the crackers are golden brown and crisp, about 15 minutes. Allow them to cool a bit on the baking sheet before serving. Store the crackers in an airtight container in the fridge, or at room temperature for up to 1 week.

Store the "puppy chow" in an airtight container in the fridge for up to 1 week.

dark chocolate nutty
puppy chow

Known as "puppy chow" (or "muddy buddies" where I grew up), this crunchy treat is Rice Chex cereal coated in peanut butter, chocolate, and confectioners' sugar. Here you will be making your own cereal from almond flour (it is easier than it sounds) and coating it in a creamy nut butter and coconut sugar-sweetened topping.

MAKES 4 CUPS

Cereal

2 cups blanched **almond flour**

½ cup plus 2 tablespoons **gluten-free tapioca flour**

2 tablespoons **flaxseed meal**

2 teaspoons **DIY Paleo Baking Powder (page 29)**

⅓ cup **coconut oil**

1 teaspoon **pure vanilla extract**

3 tablespoons **pure maple syrup**

2 tablespoons **unsweetened nondairy milk**

Chocolate Coating

¼ cup **creamy nut butter**

⅓ cup **dairy-free dark chocolate chips**

1 tablespoon **coconut oil**

Sugar Coating

¾ cup **coconut sugar**

1 tablespoon **gluten-free tapioca flour**

1. **Make the cereal:** Preheat the oven to 350°F and line two baking sheets with parchment paper.

2. In a large bowl, mix together the almond flour, tapioca flour, flaxseed meal, and baking powder. Add the coconut oil, vanilla, maple syrup, and nondairy milk and mix well with a spatula until a dough forms.

3. Place a piece of parchment paper on a flat surface and dump the dough on top. Cover it with another piece of parchment, and roll out the dough with a rolling pin to make a large rectangle about ½ inch thick.

3. Cut the dough into 1-inch squares. Transfer to the baking sheets, spacing them so they aren't touching.

4. Bake for about 8 minutes. Flip the squares and switch the baking sheets between the racks. Cook until crispy, 3 to 5 minutes more. Let the squares cool on the sheets.

5. **Make the chocolate coating:** In a small saucepan, melt the nut butter, dark chocolate, and coconut oil over low heat, stirring frequently, until fully combined. Remove the pan from the heat.

6. **Make the sugar coating:** In a small bowl, mix together the coconut sugar and tapioca flour.

7. Transfer the cereal to a large bowl. Pour the chocolate coating over top and toss with a spatula. Add the sugar coating and mix well. Allow the mixture to set, then start snacking!

crunchy baked
cinnamon churro chips

Crunchy chips coated in cinnamon and coconut sugar that taste like a churro? Um, hi, these are heavenly. Flavored churro-style—with coconut sugar, cinnamon, and some coconut oil—they're like a sweet version of a tortilla chip. These are beyond delicious when dipped in nut butter or coconut yogurt, too.

MAKES 3 CUPS

¼ cup **liquid coconut oil**

¼ cup **coconut sugar**

1 teaspoon **ground cinnamon**

5 medium **grain-free tortillas**

1. Preheat the oven to 400°F and line a baking sheet with parchment paper.

2. Pour the coconut oil into a wide shallow bowl. In another shallow bowl, mix together the coconut sugar and cinnamon.

3. One at a time, dip each tortilla into the coconut oil, coating both sides and letting the excess drip off, then dredge it in the cinnamon sugar.

4. Slice each tortilla into six equal wedges and set them on the prepared baking sheet.

5. Bake until crispy, about 10 minutes. Serve immediately. Store leftovers in an airtight container at room temperature for up to 5 days.

Want to save time in the morning? Both the dough and the blueberry jam can be prepared the night before you plan to put the tarts together and bake them.

homemade grain-free frosted
blueberry pastry tarts

Pop-Tarts, I love you more than you can imagine. When I was growing up, all I wanted to eat was blueberry Pop-Tarts—the ones with the white frosting and sprinkles on top. Never the ones without frosting, because where's the fun in that? My mom (being the smart woman she is) did not buy these for me, but luckily friends had them in stock, as did the cafeteria at school. This homemade version is dedicated to all my fellow Pop-Tart-loving friends out there. I hope they satisfy your cravings as much as they do mine!

MAKES 5 TARTS

Dough

1 cup blanched **almond flour**

1 cup **gluten-free tapioca flour**

5 tablespoons grass-fed **butter**, at room temperature

¼ cup **coconut sugar**

1 large pasture-raised **egg**

½ teaspoon **ground cinnamon**

Liquid **coconut oil**, for brushing

Blueberry Chia Jam

1 cup frozen **blueberries**

1 tablespoon **pure maple syrup**

2 tablespoons **fresh lemon juice**

2 tablespoons **chia seeds**

Coconut Glaze

1 (13-ounce) can **full-fat coconut milk**, chilled

1 tablespoon **pure maple syrup**

1. **Make the dough:** In a medium bowl, mix together the almond flour, tapioca flour, and butter with an electric hand mixer until combined. Add the coconut sugar, egg, and cinnamon and mix until a dough forms. Chill the dough in the fridge for at least 1 hour or overnight (no cover necessary).

2. **Make the blueberry chia jam:** Add the blueberries and maple syrup to a small saucepan set over medium heat. Mash the berries with a fork as they start to soften, about 5 minutes. Add the lemon juice and chia seeds and cook for a couple of minutes more, until the jam thickens. Remove the jam from the heat and let it cool completely (this step can be done the night before assembling the pastries).

3. Once the dough has chilled, preheat the oven to 350°F.

4. Place the dough on a large piece of parchment paper on a countertop. Add a second piece of parchment on top, and roll the dough out to make a large rectangle about ¼ inch thick.

recipe continues

Not craving blueberries?
Use your favorite berry!
Strawberries, raspberries,
or blackberries would
all work.

5. Remove the top piece of parchment and slice the dough into 10 equal rectangles. (Dimensions have varied for me per batch, so as long as it's 10 equal rectangles, you are good!)

6. Line a baking sheet with parchment paper (you can use the top sheet from rolling out the dough).

7. Transfer 5 of the dough rectangles to the baking sheet, spacing them about 1 inch apart, and scoop a generous tablespoon of the cooled jam onto the center of each rectangle.

8. Lightly brush the edges of each rectangle with coconut oil. Add another piece of dough on top and press lightly with your fingers along the edges to enclose the jam. Crimp the edges with a fork to seal them.

9. Bake until just about golden, 12 to 15 minutes. Let the tarts cool on the baking sheet.

10. **While the tarts are cooling, make the glaze:** Scoop the top layer of thick coconut cream out of the can of coconut milk and put it into a large bowl. Add the maple syrup and cream with an electric hand mixer until the glaze is smooth and fully combined.

11. Once the tarts are cool, spread the glaze on top of each one and dollop with any extra jam, if desired. Serve warm or at room temperature. Extra tarts will keep in an airtight container in the freezer for up to 2 months. Let them thaw at room temperature or in a low oven.

toasted coconut **marshmallows**

I know, I know—a marshmallow recipe that is paleo sounds like an oxymoron, but go with me on this, you guys. S'mores are one of my favorite desserts in the whole world (see page 96), and creating my own marshmallow recipe has been on my list for far too long. I have always been intimidated to make them, but these are by far a hundred times easier than I expected them to be. Unlike your traditional mallow, there's no refined sugar in them, and they toast up just as golden as the ones you grew up with.

MAKES 20 TO 24

½ teaspoon coconut oil

¼ cup toasted coconut flakes (optional)

3 tablespoons grass-fed beef gelatin

1 cup filtered water

1 cup pure maple syrup

1 teaspoon pure vanilla extract

1. Grease an 8 × 8-inch baking pan with coconut oil and line it with parchment paper. Sprinkle half of the toasted coconut flakes across the pan.

2. In a large bowl, combine the gelatin and ½ cup of the water.

3. In a small saucepan over medium-high heat, add the remaining ½ cup water, the maple syrup, and vanilla and bring to a boil. Reduce the heat to medium-low and cook, stirring every minute or so, until full combined (it won't be thick), about 8 minutes.

4. Remove the saucepan from the heat and pour the mixture into the bowl with the gelatin. Using a hand mixer on medium-high speed, beat the mixture until it becomes thick like marshmallow fluff. Pour the mixture into the prepared pan and smooth the top with a spatula. Sprinkle the remaining coconut flakes on top. Allow the fluff to set at room temperature, 4 to 6 hours up to overnight (which is best).

5. Using the edges of the parchment paper, lift the set marshmallow from the pan, and slice it into about twenty-four 1-inch squares. Store the marshmallows in an airtight container for 5 to 7 days at room temperature. (Do not freeze or store in the refrigerator.)

grain-free **cinnamon sugar graham crackers**

Who here loves making s'mores? They are always a crowd favorite in my world. Melty marshmallow (toasted until golden is my preference) on top of a piece of dark chocolate sandwiched between two crispy, crunchy cinnamon graham crackers? *Yum.* This recipe will take your graham cracker game to the next level—refined sugar-free, grain-free, and so flavorful. The crackers make for the most delicious s'mores but are also craveable on their own as a sweet and crunchy snack.

MAKES ABOUT 20 CRACKERS

2 cups blanched **almond flour**

⅓ cup plus 2 tablespoons **coconut sugar**

1 teaspoon **DIY Paleo Baking Powder** (page 29)

2 tablespoons **coconut oil** or grass-fed **butter**, melted

1 large pasture-raised **egg**

1 teaspoon **pure vanilla extract**

2 teaspoons **ground cinnamon**

To turn your graham crackers into s'mores, as pictured, use dairy-free dark chocolate and the Toasted Coconut Marshmallows (skip the coconut, if you like) on page 95.

1. Preheat the oven to 300°F.

2. In a large bowl, mix together the almond flour, ⅓ cup coconut sugar, and the baking powder. Add the melted butter, egg, and vanilla and mix again until well combined.

3. Form the dough with your hands into a ball and transfer it to a surface lined with a large sheet of parchment paper. Top with another large piece of parchment paper. Roll out the dough with a rolling pin or a glass bottle to make a large rectangle about ¼ inch thick, and remove the top piece of parchment.

4. In a small bowl, mix together the cinnamon and the remaining 2 tablespoons coconut sugar. Sprinkle the cinnamon-sugar mixture over the cracker dough.

5. Slice the dough into 2-inch squares with a knife or a cookie cutter. Poke each cracker with fork, if desired.

6. Without moving the crackers, gently transfer the parchment paper onto a baking sheet.

7. Bake until the crackers are golden around the edges, 20 to 25 minutes.

8. Let the crackers cool and crisp up on the baking sheet for about 30 minutes before serving. Store the crackers in an airtight container at room temperature for up to 5 days.

peanut butter cup **protein bars**

All of your dreams came true in this bar. Peanut butter plus chocolate plus a satisfying protein-filled snack? Okay, okay, we can now snack in peace. These vegan bars—grain-free and filled with plant-based protein powder—will satisfy your sweet tooth despite having zero added sugar. Bonus: you will also save some cash by making your own snack bars instead of stocking up at the store!

MAKES 12 BARS

2 teaspoons **liquid coconut oil**

¾ cup creamy **peanut butter**

1 teaspoon **pure vanilla extract**

½ cup **flaxseed meal**

½ cup vanilla plant-based **protein powder** (Garden of Life is my fave)

¼ cup **tahini**

3 tablespoons blanched **almond flour**

1½ tablespoons **cacao powder**

Nut-free? Sub ½ cup oat or spelt flour for the almond flour, and sunflower butter or tahini for the peanut butter.

1. Line an 8-inch square baking dish with parchment paper.

2. In a small saucepan, combine the coconut oil, peanut butter, and vanilla. Heat over low heat, stirring frequently, until melted and well combined, 1 to 2 minutes. Remove the pan from the heat and let the mixture cool for a few minutes.

3. Add the flaxseed meal and protein powder to a large bowl and mix well. Pour the peanut butter mixture into the bowl and stir with a spatula until well combined. Pour the mixture into the prepared baking dish and spread it out evenly.

4. In a separate small saucepan, combine the tahini, almond flour, and cacao powder and warm over medium heat until well combined.

5. Pour the tahini mixture over the peanut butter layer and spread it out evenly with a spatula.

6. Freeze until set, about 30 minutes, and cut it into 12 bars. Store the bars in an airtight container in the fridge for up to 1 week, or in the freezer for a couple of months.

marshmallow-less
crispy rice treats

When I was in college, you could find me eating a microwaved homemade version of a Rice Krispies Treat after lunch pretty much every day. (Ten seconds was perfect to warm it up and get the marshmallow to ooze out.) These days, I make these sweet marshmallow-less treats and they always hit the spot. These bites are even Dad-approved, so you know they must be good. (He is the Sweet Tooth King of Classic Desserts and usually prefers the real thing over the "healthified" version.) You can find us both eating these straight from the pan when I make them—they're too good!

MAKES 9 BARS

2½ cups **brown rice crisps cereal**

¼ cup **cacao nibs**

½ cup **creamy nut butter**, plus more (optional) for drizzling

⅓ cup **pure maple syrup**

3 tablespoons **liquid coconut oil**

Melted **dairy-free dark chocolate**, for drizzling (optional)

1. Line an 8-inch square baking dish with parchment paper.

2. In a large bowl, stir together the brown rice cereal and cacao nibs.

3. In a small saucepan, combine the nut butter, maple syrup, and coconut oil. Stir constantly over low heat until melted (don't let it burn), 1 to 3 minutes.

4. Pour the melted nut butter mixture into the bowl and mix until the rice crisps are coated.

5. Transfer the treat mixture to the prepared baking dish and press down on it with a spatula in an even layer.

6. Chill the mixture in the fridge until set, about 1 hour. Slice it into 9 bars and drizzle some nut butter or melted chocolate on top, if desired.

Nut-free? Sub sunflower butter or tahini for the nut butter. I don't recommend coconut butter because it will be too liquid when you melt it.

ultimate chewy **granola bars**

We are combining two of life's greatest foods in this recipe: sweet potato and banana. If I had to pick one veggie and one fruit to use in every recipe for the rest of my life, it would be sweet potatoes and bananas. They're inexpensive, so easy to bake and cook with, and add the best consistency and moisture to baked goods. I know the word *moisture* can gross some of us out, but it is true! These sweet-potato-meets-banana-bread granola bars make for a delicious sweet snack to get you through the afternoon slump—or you can crumble one up and add it to your breakfast bowl.

MAKES 12 BARS

½ teaspoon **coconut oil**, plus more for greasing the baking dish

2 cups sprouted **gluten-free rolled oats**

½ cup **gluten-free oat flour**

2 tablespoons **flaxseed**

2 tablespoons **chia seeds**

1 teaspoon **ground cinnamon**

½ cup mashed **banana** (about 1 medium banana)

½ cup **sweet potato puree** (see page 238)

2 tablespoons **pure maple syrup**

½ cup **unsweetened nondairy milk**

⅓ cup **creamy seed butter**

1 teaspoon **pure vanilla extract**

⅓ cup plus 3 tablespoons **dairy-free dark chocolate chips**

1. Preheat the oven to 350°F and grease an 8-inch square baking dish with coconut oil.

2. In a large bowl, mix together the oats, oat flour, flaxseed, chia seeds, and cinnamon. Add the mashed banana, sweet potato puree, maple syrup, nondairy milk, seed butter, and vanilla and mix again until well combined. Fold in ⅓ cup dark chocolate chips.

3. Transfer the dough to the prepared baking dish, pressing down on it with a spatula to flatten it.

4. Bake until the bar is set and cooked through, 20 to 25 minutes. Remove the baking dish from the oven and let the bar cool in the dish for about 15 minutes.

5. Melt the coconut oil and the remaining 3 tablespoons dark chocolate chips together in the microwave or in a small sauté pan set over low heat. Stir until well combined.

6. Drizzle the chocolate over the granola bar. Slice into 12 bars and enjoy. The bars will keep in an airtight container at room temperature for up to 5 days, or in the freezer for up to 2 months.

Looking for a snack to take to work? These are super easy to pack in a container. I add a little nut butter on top, and fresh fruit when I'm feeling fancy.

extra-comfort food

Your New Form of Self-Care: Food to Fuel Your Soul

You're never really prepared for the feeling you get when you're fired from your job. Especially when you are twenty-five years old and feeling pretty good about your life. I had just married Jordan a couple of months prior and was absolutely loving my newfound hobby of making recipes. In just a matter of minutes, though, everything changed. After sitting through an all-day meeting, I was pulled into another room and was fired. I left what was likely the most uncomfortable meeting of my life, headed out of the building, and called my dad (cue the waterworks). I started to walk to our apartment, figuring out how to break it to Jord that his new wife was now unemployed.

There is really no "good time" of the year to lose your job, but I do think that December has to be one of the toughest. Everyone is watching *Home Alone 2*, shopping for presents, eating platters of cookies, and enjoying themselves, as they should. Meanwhile, I was at home, thinking the world was ending. I could barely see the littlest spec of light at the end of this scary tunnel. What the [*bleep*] was I going to do? Sure, I blogged on the side, but how was I going to make a living from that? I was making $50 a post at the time. In Manhattan, that could maybe cover a dinner or two out with friends.

Nothing but comfort foods for the soul here, friends

A few weeks into the unemployed life, I was sitting at a pizza place having dinner with Jord and my parents. They each nudged me to go out on my own and build something from my blog. They said, "Give yourself three to six months and see what happens." They pushed me to follow my passion and do what I love, something I didn't have faith in at the time. But that is exactly what I attempted.

And it worked out. In the most amazing and unexpected way possible. Looking back, I am the first to say (or really, my mom is—hi, Mom) that losing my job was a complete blessing in disguise. It took a ton of hard work, perseverance, and tenacity, but I got here.

Everyone goes through rough times in their career and in life in general: a bad breakup, a personal crisis, or just a phase of feeling out of it. Those times don't call for green juice and chopped salads—you call in the "big guys" when you need comfort. In this chapter, you'll find my favorite recipes for the days when the trials and tribulations strike and you want a comforting meal that's still good for you, like Chili Mac + Cheese with Corn-Less Cornbread (page 122). Or what about some Sweet Potato Chip Nachos with Jalapeño Cashew Cheese (page 109)? Nothing but comfort foods for the soul here, friends.

Looking to serve these with a meal? They go well with Jord's Sunday Roasted Chicken (page 128).

homemade **sweet potato pierogis**

This recipe is dedicated to my best friend from college: Marls, I know your love for pierogis is real. I wasn't a huge pierogi fan until I got on the sweet potato train, and now I am all about these potato dumplings. They are egg-free and gluten-free, and I cannot wait to hear what you think of them.

A warning: this is the most labor-intensive recipe in the whole book. And by labor-intensive, I'm just saying it takes more effort than stirring eggs to make a scramble. I promise it is simple, but since you're making all the components from scratch, just have patience and some fun with it. Put on a favorite podcast or some music and get lost in the kitchen. (These are great to freeze and save for later, too.)

MAKES 20 TO 25 PIEROGIS

Dough

3 cups **gluten-free oat flour**, plus more for dusting

½ teaspoon **sea salt**

¼ cup (½ stick) grass-fed **butter**, melted

1 tablespoon **avocado oil**

Filling

1 small **sweet potato**, peeled and diced

½ medium **onion**, chopped

Avocado oil, for cooking

3 tablespoons **unsweetened nondairy milk**

2 teaspoons **nutritional yeast**

1 teaspoon **apple cider vinegar**

1 **garlic clove**, minced

Sea salt and freshly ground black pepper

Unsweetened applesauce, for serving

Coconut yogurt, for serving

1. **Make the dough:** In a large bowl, combine the oat flour and salt and mix well. Add 1 cup of water and the melted butter, and stir until the dough comes together.

2. Transfer the dough to a lightly floured surface and knead it a few times until smooth, adding a little more flour as needed.

3. Place the dough in a clean medium bowl and drizzle it with the avocado oil to prevent sticking. Let the dough sit for about 1 hour at room temperature.

4. **Meanwhile, make the filling:** Place the sweet potato in a medium pot and add cold water to cover. Bring the water to a boil and cook until the sweet potato is tender, about 15 minutes; then drain.

5. Place the onion in a large skillet. Drizzle avocado oil on top and cook over medium heat, stirring often, until the onion is starting to brown, 5 to 7 minutes. Cover the skillet and reduce the heat to low. Cook, stirring every 5 minutes or so, until the onion is softened and well browned, about 15 minutes.

6. Transfer the sweet potato to a large bowl and mash it with a fork until smooth. Add the nondairy milk, nutritional yeast, apple cider vinegar, and garlic. Mix

recipe continues

in the cooked onion and stir until combined. Season with salt and pepper to taste.

7. Divide the dough in half and roll out one portion on a lightly floured surface to make a square ⅛ to ¼ inch thick. Cut out 3-inch rounds using a cookie cutter or a drinking glass. Repeat with the second portion.

8. Place ½ to 1 tablespoon of the potato mixture on the center of each dough round and swipe around the edges of the dough with a damp paper towel to wet the dough slightly. Fold the rounds in half and seal the edges together with a fork. Flip and seal on the other side as well. Make sure the edges are sealed well so they won't fall apart! Chill the pierogis in the fridge for 10 to 15 minutes.

9. Fill a large pot with water and bring it to a boil. Add a handful of the pierogis (the number will vary based on the pot size, but don't crowd them!) and cook until they float to the surface, 4 to 6 minutes. Remove them with a slotted spoon and repeat with the remaining pierogis.

10. Grease a large skillet with avocado oil and heat it over medium heat. Transfer the boiled pierogis to the skillet and crisp until golden brown, about 3 minutes on each side. Serve them warm, with applesauce or coconut yogurt alongside. Any extra cooked pierogis will keep in an airtight container in the freezer for up to 2 months. Reheat them in a skillet that you have greased with avocado oil, grass-fed butter, or ghee.

Have leftover filling? Save it and add it to an omelet or smear it on toast!

sweet potato chip nachos
with jalapeño cashew "cheese"

As a self-proclaimed sweet potato addict, I believe there are no limits when it comes to using sweet potatoes in the kitchen. For example, here's an easy way to turn sweet potatoes into a nacho chip base for this platter of heaven. And it gets better. We top it off not with your usual nacho cheese, but with a homemade jalapeño cashew "cheese," making this recipe vegan, paleo, and a guaranteed crowd-pleaser. This is a delicious and easy recipe to serve friends. Just double the recipe for eight guests or triple it for a party of twelve.

SERVES 4

3 large **sweet potatoes** (1 to 2 pounds total), scrubbed

1 tablespoon **avocado oil**

Sea salt and **freshly ground black pepper**

Jalapeño Cashew "Cheese" (recipe follows)

⅓ cup **salsa**

1 medium **avocado**, peeled, pitted, and diced

¼ cup chopped **onion**

1 small **jalapeño**, sliced

Small bunch of **fresh cilantro**, chopped

1. Preheat the oven to 425°F and line a baking sheet with parchment paper.

2. Slice the sweet potatoes into ¼-inch-thick rounds and put them into a large bowl. Add the avocado oil and salt and pepper to taste, and toss.

3. Transfer the sweet potato rounds to the prepared baking sheet and bake, flipping them halfway through, until they are starting to brown around the edges, about 30 minutes.

4. When the sweet potatoes have finished baking, turn on the broiler and broil the chips for about 1 minute to crisp them.

5. Transfer the sweet potato chips to a serving platter, if desired, or leave them on the baking sheet. Top with the cashew "cheese," salsa, avocado, onion, jalapeño, and cilantro.

recipe continues

Want to add some protein on top? Grass-fed beef crumbles and shredded chicken are both delicious with these nachos!

Craving real chips instead of sweet potatoes? Sub in your favorite tortilla chips.

jalapeño cashew "cheese"

MAKES 1 CUP

1 cup **raw cashews**

1 cup boiling **filtered water**,
plus ½ cup hot **filtered water**
(or more as needed)

3 tablespoons **nutritional yeast**

½ teaspoon **chili powder**

½ teaspoon **garlic powder**

½ teaspoon **sea salt**

½ small **jalapeño**, seeded and
chopped

1. Place the raw cashews in a small heatproof bowl and cover them with the boiling water. Let them soak for 20 minutes.

2. Strain the cashews, transfer them to a food processor, and add the nutritional yeast, chili powder, garlic powder, salt, and jalapeño. Blend until creamy. Add the hot water and blend again until smooth. If the mixture is too thick, add 2 tablespoons of hot water at a time until it reaches the desired consistency. The cheese will keep in the fridge for up to 1 week.

Not a fan of jalapeño? Use fresh chives or scallions instead.

vegan "chicken" + waffles

Whenever my dad went away on a business trip, my mom would sneak us fried chicken for dinner. She is probably going to be upset that our little secret is out when she sees this, but it still makes me laugh. She loves fried chicken and Dad, being the dedicated health guru when we were growing up, was in no way eating fried chicken for dinner. We used to love eating it cold instead of hot and would pick the crispy skin off and save it for last. This "chicken" and waffles is a lightened-up vegan version of the comfort-food staple. Don't forget to pour some maple syrup on top to round out the whole meal.

SERVES 4 OR 5

Fried Cauliflower "Chicken"

4 tablespoons **unsweetened nondairy milk**

½ cup **hot sauce**

3 **flax eggs** (see page 29)

2 cups **gluten-free oat flour**

2 teaspoons **baking powder**

1 teaspoon **freshly ground black pepper**

1 teaspoon **sea salt**

3 tablespoons **avocado oil**

½ medium head **cauliflower,** cored and cut into small florets

Waffles (recipe follows)

Pure maple syrup, for serving

1. In a medium bowl, mix together the nondairy milk, hot sauce, and flax eggs until well combined.

2. In a separate shallow bowl, mix the oat flour, baking powder, pepper, and salt.

3. Heat the avocado oil in a large skillet over medium-low heat until it is hot, then increase the heat to medium.

4. Dip a few of the cauliflower florets in the hot sauce mixture and toss them in the flour mixture, coating them well. Add them to the hot oil and fry until golden brown, about 5 minutes. Transfer the fried cauliflower to a paper towel–lined plate to drain. Repeat for all the cauliflower pieces.

5. Serve warm, with the waffles and maple syrup.

This recipe tastes best when eaten right away. I don't recommend making it more than an hour before serving.

waffles

MAKES 4 OR 5 WAFFLES

Avocado oil, for greasing
the waffle iron

1½ cups **gluten-free oat flour**

2 tablespoons **baking powder**

1 tablespoon **coconut sugar**

1 cup **unsweetened
nondairy milk**

1. Heat a waffle iron according to the manufacturer's instructions and grease it with avocado oil.

2. In a large bowl, whisk together the oat flour, baking powder, and coconut sugar. Add the nondairy milk and whisk to combine. Let the batter sit for about 5 minutes.

3. Spoon ¼ cup of the batter into the waffle iron and cook according to the manufacturer's instructions, until golden and fluffy. Repeat with the remaining batter. Serve warm.

oven-baked **veggie tots**

Did anyone else love getting hash browns at McDonald's when their mom wasn't around? These oven-baked veggie tots will take you right back to those days. Dip them into your favorite ketchup or mustard, enjoy them with scrambled eggs, or just pop them in your mouth like Tic Tacs. Filled with sweet potatoes, zucchini, and spices, these gems are so easy to make, you'll be wondering why you haven't been eating them your whole life. (Sorry-not-sorry, McDonald's!)

MAKES ABOUT 20 TOTS

2 medium **sweet potatoes,** peeled and cut in half crosswize

2 medium **zucchini**

1 teaspoon **garlic powder**

½ teaspoon **sea salt**

½ teaspoon **freshly ground black pepper**

1 tablespoon **coconut flour**

1 to 2 tablespoons **avocado oil**

> **Don't have sweet potatoes?** Feel free to use white potatoes, too! Any large potatoes will work.

1. Add the sweet potatoes to a large pot filled with cold water. Bring the water to a boil and cook until the sweet potatoes are tender but not too mushy, 25 to 30 minutes. Strain the sweet potatoes and let them cool a bit (you can rinse them under cold water to expedite this).

2. Add the sweet potatoes to a large bowl and mash them well with a fork until they are smooth and no lumps remain.

3. Grate the zucchini on the large holes of a box grater. Wrap the grated zucchini in paper towels and squeeze out any excess liquid (you should end up with about 2 cups of zucchini). Add the zucchini to the bowl containing the sweet potatoes, and sprinkle with the garlic powder, salt, pepper, and coconut flour.

4. Using a spatula or fork, mix everything together. Chill the mixture in the fridge for 15 to 30 minutes.

5. Preheat the oven to 425°F. Line a baking sheet with parchment paper and grease the paper with a bit of the avocado oil.

6. Using your hands, form each tot from about 2 tablespoons of the sweet potato mixture. Place the tots on the prepared baking sheet and drizzle avocado oil on top of them (this will help them crisp).

7. Bake for about 20 minutes. Turn the tots over, drizzle a bit more avocado oil on top and bake until golden, about 15 minutes more. Serve warm.

crispy oven-baked **frickles**

Raise your hand if you love fried pickles (both my hands are raised). There is no stopping my love for pickle-anything, but frickles take it to a whole new level. Salty with a little crunch, these crispy frickles are the best side dish for burger night. Dip them into the spicy aioli here or into some honey mustard.

SERVES 4 OR 5

Batter

⅓ cup **unsweetened nondairy milk**

1 tablespoon blanched **almond flour**

¼ teaspoon **garlic powder**

1 tablespoon **nutritional yeast**

Crispy Coating

½ cup **grain-free bread crumbs** (see page 29)

¼ cup blanched **almond flour**

1 tablespoon **nutritional yeast**

¼ teaspoon **sea salt**

½ teaspoon **freshly ground black pepper**

Pickles

5 large lacto-fermented **pickles**, sliced into 1-inch-thick rounds

Spicy Aioli

⅓ cup **mayonnaise** (paleo or vegan, if needed)

1 tablespoon **Sriracha** or other **hot sauce**

Sea salt and **freshly ground black pepper**

½ teaspoon **garlic powder**

1. Preheat the oven to 425°F and line a baking sheet with parchment paper.

2. **Make the batter:** In a medium bowl, whisk together the nondairy milk, almond flour, garlic powder, and nutritional yeast.

3. **Make the crispy coating:** Combine the bread crumbs, almond flour, nutritional yeast, salt, and pepper in a medium bowl and mix well.

4. One at a time, dip each pickle round into the batter, then into the crispy coating, and place on the prepared baking sheet. Bake until golden, about 5 minutes. Flip and bake for about 5 minutes more.

5. **While the pickles bake, make the spicy aioli:** Mix the mayo, Sriracha, ½ teaspoon pepper, and garlic powder together in a small bowl. Season with salt to taste.

6. Serve the pickles warm, with the spicy aioli for dipping. Leftovers will keep in an airtight container in the fridge for 5 days. Reheat them in the oven at 425°F or in a greased skillet over medium-high heat.

Don't eat butter?
Sub the vegan butter
of your choice! Just
make sure it is softened
a bit to a ghee-like
consistency. Coconut
oil does not work well
in this recipe.

gluten-free homemade **biscuits**

Warm biscuits straight out of the oven, smeared with a little grass-fed butter and homemade jam. Please tell me your mouth just watered, because mine sure did. These homemade biscuits are a go-to when we want something bready to dip into our chili or when we want to bring a great side dish for a holiday meal. They are even Jord-approved—he is the biscuit king, to say the least. Try toasting one and adding blueberry jam (see page 93) with creamy peanut butter for the ultimate classic combo.

MAKES 8 BISCUITS

¾ cup **unsweetened nondairy milk**

1 tablespoon **apple cider vinegar**

1 cup **gluten-free oat flour**, plus more for dusting

1 cup blanched **almond flour**

2 tablespoons **gluten-free tapioca flour**

½ teaspoon **sea salt**

3 teaspoons **baking powder**

3 tablespoons grass-fed **butter**, at room temperature

Avocado oil, **ghee**, or melted **butter**, for brushing

1. Preheat the oven to 400°F and line a baking sheet with parchment paper.

2. In a small bowl or liquid measuring cup, combine the nondairy milk and apple cider vinegar.

3. In a large bowl, combine the oat flour, almond flour, tapioca flour, salt, and baking powder and mix well.

4. Add the butter to the dry ingredients, and cut it into the flour with a fork until small pieces form.

5. Add the wet ingredients to the dry ingredients and stir well. The dough will be sticky and a little wet.

6. Transfer the dough to a well-floured surface and sprinkle more flour on top of the dough (2 to 3 tablespoons, depending on how wet the dough is).

7. Form the dough into a disk that's about 3 inches thick, and slice the disk into 8 pieces with a knife. Form each piece into a biscuit shape (round or square).

8. Transfer the biscuits to the prepared baking sheet, leaving about 1 inch between them, and brush the tops with avocado oil.

9. Bake until the biscuits are just golden, 18 to 20 minutes. Serve warm. Leftover biscuits will keep in an airtight container at room temperature for 2 days or in the freezer for up to 2 months. Reheat in the oven or microwave once thawed.

extra-comfort food

japanese sweet potato latkes
with cashew sour cream

Potato latkes have been a staple at every Hanukkah dinner in my family since I was little. Jord is a self-proclaimed potato peeler and loves helping my mom make them. Latkes will most definitely stink up your kitchen and your hair when you're frying them, but if you love them, they are well worth the trouble. I created this version with grated Japanese sweet potatoes, which are a complete game changer for making latkes. Whether you celebrate Hanukkah or not, no one needs a holiday as an excuse to make these potato pancakes. Dipped into a homemade cashew sour cream, they're simply dreamy. Enjoy these latkes with any meal, any time of the year!

SERVES 4 OR 5

2 large **Japanese sweet potatoes** (1 to 1½ pounds total), scrubbed

3 large pasture-raised **eggs**

½ teaspoon **smoked paprika**

½ teaspoon **freshly ground black pepper**

½ cup chopped **onion**

1 tablespoon **gluten-free tapioca flour**

Avocado oil, for frying

Sea salt

Cashew Sour Cream (recipe follows)

1. Grate the sweet potatoes using the grater blade in a food processor or on the large holes of a box grater. Wrap the grated sweet potato in paper towels and squeeze out any excess moisture.

2. In a large bowl, whisk together the eggs, paprika, and pepper. Add the onion, tapioca flour, and sweet potatoes. Mix well.

3. Add a splash of avocado oil to a large skillet and heat it over medium heat.

4. Using a spoon, scoop a generous tablespoon of the batter onto the skillet and flatten it a bit with the back of the spoon. Add more batter to the skillet, but don't overcrowd the latkes. Cook the latkes until crispy, about 3 minutes on each side. As they are cooked, transfer them to a plate lined with paper towels to drain. Season the latkes with salt to taste.

5. Serve the latkes hot, with the sour cream alongside.

cashew sour cream

MAKES ABOUT 1 CUP

1 cup **raw cashews**

1 cup boiling **filtered water**

½ cup **unsweetened nondairy milk**

1 teaspoon **apple cider vinegar**

3 tablespoons **fresh lemon juice**

1. Add the cashews to a small heatproof bowl, cover them with the boiling water, and let them soak for 20 minutes.

2. Strain the cashews and place them in a blender. Add the nondairy milk, apple cider vinegar, and lemon juice, and blend until very smooth. The cashew sour cream will keep in the fridge for 5 days.

Can't find Japanese sweet potatoes? Sub any large potato you'd like. White and regular sweet potatoes are both delicious.

corn-less cornbread

MAKES ONE 8-INCH SQUARE LOAF

2 tablespoons liquid **coconut oil**, plus more for greasing the baking dish

1 cup blanched **almond flour**

⅓ cup **coconut flour**

2 teaspoons **baking powder**

3 pasture-raised **eggs**, at room temperature

¼ cup **pure maple syrup**

½ cup **unsweetened nondairy milk**

1. Preheat the oven to 350°F and grease an 8-inch square baking dish with coconut oil.

2. Mix the almond flour, coconut flour, and baking powder together in a large bowl. Add the eggs, coconut oil, maple syrup, and nondairy milk and mix until creamy and well combined.

3. Pour the batter into the prepared baking dish. Bake until the bread is golden brown and a toothpick inserted in the center comes out clean, 25 to 30 minutes.

4. Let the bread cool for a few minutes in the pan, then cut it into 9 pieces. Serve with the chili mac and cheese. Leftover cornbread will keep well in an airtight container on the counter for 2 days or in the fridge for up to 5 days. You can also freeze it for up to 2 months. Rewarm it in the oven on a baking sheet at 350°F or microwave.

chili mac + cheese
with corn-less cornbread

When I used to go to a BBQ place near my childhood home, I would always get the cornbread muffins. These days, I don't do much corn unless it's on the cob from the local farm, or maybe corn tortilla chips at a restaurant, so when I made this corn-free "cornbread" to go with chili mac and cheese and it actually tasted like the real thing, I was on cloud nine. (J didn't even know there wasn't corn in it.) Dipped into the creamy, cheesy sauce in the macaroni, it is beyond comfort-food heaven.

SERVES 4

12 ounces **gluten-free short pasta** (such as elbows or small shells)

¾ cup **raw cashews**

1½ cups boiling **filtered water**

1 tablespoon **avocado oil**

½ white **onion**, chopped

3 **garlic cloves**, minced

1 cup **bone broth** or **veggie broth**

½ cup **unsweetened nondairy milk**

1 tablespoon **gluten-free tapioca flour**

½ teaspoon **ground cumin**

¾ teaspoon **chili powder**

½ teaspoon **freshly ground black pepper**

½ teaspoon **sea salt**

2 tablespoons **nutritional yeast**

¼ cup diced **chiles**

Corn-Less Cornbread (recipe opposite)

1. Bring a large pot of salted water to a boil and cook the pasta according to the package instructions. Drain the pasta and place it in a baking dish.

2. While the pasta cooks, place the cashews in a medium heatproof bowl and cover them with the boiling water. Let the cashews soak for 20 minutes. Drain.

3. Meanwhile, heat the avocado oil in a medium skillet over medium heat. Add the onion and garlic and cook until softened, 7 to 10 minutes.

4. Transfer the cooked onion and garlic to a blender, and add the drained cashews, broth, nondairy milk, tapioca flour, cumin, chili powder, black pepper, salt, and nutritional yeast. Blend on medium-high speed until smooth and creamy.

5. Pour the sauce over the cooked pasta and top it with the diced chiles. Serve warm with the cornbread. Leftover mac and cheese will keep in an airtight container in the fridge for up to 5 days. Add a splash of water or nondairy milk to the chili mac and warm it in a microwave.

I love using bone broth in this recipe for the extra collagen and flavor, but feel free to use any broth you prefer!

not-so-piggy **pigs in a blanket**

When Jord and I were planning our wedding, he had one request. Okay, I kid, he had many more requests than that (don't underestimate the groom's opinions, friends . . .). But for J, the most important part of our reception was that we serve good old pigs in a blanket during the cocktail hour. Black-tie wedding with mini hot dogs and mustard—sounds about right. It was the first of many compromises as a married couple. Now that meat is in my life again, I was determined to make a healthier grain-free version for us. Dip them in your favorite mustard or ketchup—you will love! This recipe is a great appetizer to whip up for any game-day events (coming from the girl who falls asleep during the Super Bowl).

MAKES ABOUT 50 MINI HOT DOGS

3 cups blanched **almond flour**, plus more for dusting

¼ cup (½ stick) cold grass-fed **butter**

2 large pasture-raised **eggs**

1 teaspoon **pure maple syrup**

12 nitrate-free, uncured, fully cooked **hot dogs**, each sliced into 4 pieces

Dijon mustard or ketchup, for serving

Don't eat red meat? Sub in your favorite plant-based veggie sausage or chicken sausage.

Can't do almond flour? Sub 2¾ cups gluten-free oat flour.

1. Place the almond flour, butter, eggs, and maple syrup in a food processor and pulse until a ball of dough forms. Divide the dough into two balls, cover them in plastic wrap, and chill them in the fridge for about 20 minutes.

2. Meanwhile, preheat the oven to 400°F and line a baking sheet with parchment paper.

3. Place one of the balls of dough on a lightly floured surface and cover it with a piece of parchment paper. Roll out the dough to make a large rectangle about ⅛ inch thick (if the dough is sticky, sprinkle more flour on top as you roll it or return it to the fridge for a bit longer). Using a knife, slice the dough into 2- to 3-inch triangular pieces. Repeat with the second ball of dough.

4. Place a hot dog piece at the wide base of a dough triangle, and roll the dough up around it until the hot dog is covered. Repeat with the remaining dough and hot dogs.

5. Transfer the wrapped hot dogs to the prepared baking sheet and bake until the dough is fully cooked and just golden, 10 to 15 minutes. Serve warm, with Dijon mustard or ketchup for dipping.

meat

Bring on the Double Double: Basic Protein-Packed Recipes

Let me start by saying that I don't think there is any right or wrong when it comes to animal protein. Everyone's body is different, and it is important for each of us to remember that listening to what our own body needs is the best thing we can do for it. Try not to compare yourself with others and how they eat—just eat what makes you feel good. For some, that includes quality animal proteins, while others do better without. It doesn't make one way "good" or the other "bad." One of the best parts of being *you* is that you're the only one who will know what makes you feel your best.

A few years ago, I went through a "no meat" phase. I didn't eat any animal protein besides wild fish and pasture-raised eggs for five years. It was what my body wanted at the time (I simply woke up one morning and no longer craved meat) and I don't regret it. But after a few years, I began to learn that a meat-free life wasn't sustainable for me in the long term and I returned to the carnivore life.

This process really proved to me how much we need to listen to our bodies and also that we need to recognize that we change over time. Just because something works for us one day, that doesn't mean

> remember that listening to what our own body needs is the best thing we can do for it

it will work forever. It doesn't matter what your best friend, mom, or coworkers are eating. It only matters what you want and what works for you. If you look at something and it doesn't look good to you, don't eat it. If you see something that looks drool-worthy but no one else wants it, who cares? Eat it and *enjoy it*! Listen to your beautiful body and what it's saying to you.

For those who do favor eating meat or would like to prepare it for friends and family, I recommend being particular about where your meat is sourced from and buying only the highest quality. Look for grass-fed and grass-finished beef, organic free-range chicken with no added hormones or antibiotics, wild-caught fish, and pasture-raised eggs. The same goes for bone broth—always look for the best-quality broth to sip and cook with.

I am sharing all our favorite meat-based recipes with you in this chapter. Say hello to Jord's famous Sunday Roasted Chicken (page 129), which I cannot recommend enough. If meat isn't your thing, I totally get it and I promise there is a ton more goodness coming your way. Skip on over to page 148 or make one of these dishes for your meat-loving family or friends.

Wondering how to use some leftover chicken? Try the Epic 5-Minute Quesadilla on page 206 or the Soba Noodle Veggie Stir-Fry on page 205, or use it as a taco or panini filling. It goes well with so many things!

sunday roasted chicken by jord

Every other Sunday, Jord roasts us a whole chicken. It is juicy, tender, flavorful, and impressive enough to share with friends and family. You can enjoy it with a couple of sides or cut it up to use in tacos, pizza, sandwiches—anything! After watching Jord make this a few times, I understood that roasting your own chicken isn't as intimidating as it sounds, and it is much healthier than the store-bought version. This is one of the recipes that was a must-have in this book! I know you guys will love it as much as we do!

SERVES 4 OR 5

1 small sweet **onion**, halved

1 tablespoon **avocado oil**, plus more for drizzling

2 medium **carrots**, cut into 2- to 3-inch pieces

2 medium **celery stalks**, cut into 2- to 3-inch pieces

5 **garlic cloves**

1 whole (4- to 5-pound) hormone- and antibiotic-free **chicken**

2 **lemons**, halved

½ teaspoon **sea salt**

1 teaspoon **freshly ground black pepper**

1 teaspoon **garlic powder**

½ teaspoon **Italian seasoning**

1. Preheat the oven to 450°F.

2. Coarsely chop one of the onion halves.

3. Drizzle 1 tablespoon avocado oil in a large cast-iron skillet. Add the chopped onion, carrots, celery, and garlic.

4. Clean the chicken by removing the giblets pouch from the cavity and then running water through the cavity to make sure there is no residue left inside. Pat the chicken dry, inside and out, with paper towels.

5. Stuff the remaining onion half and one lemon half into the cavity. Place the chicken breast-side up on top of the vegetables in the skillet.

6. Drizzle some avocado oil and squeeze the 3 remaining lemon halves all over the chicken. Sprinkle with the salt, pepper, garlic powder, and Italian seasoning, and rub the spices into the chicken.

7. Roast the chicken for 20 minutes. Reduce the oven temperature to 350°F and cook until a meat thermometer inserted in the thickest part of the thigh registers 165°F, another 10 to 12 minutes per pound, for a total of 40 to 60 minutes.

8. Let the chicken rest for a few minutes before carving and serving. You can discard the veggies or enjoy them with the chicken. (Jord loves the carrots!) Store any leftovers in an airtight container in the fridge for up to 5 days.

ginger-scallion turkey burgers
with spicy coconut peanut sauce

Turkey burgers are a weekly staple over here. They're perfect for lunch or dinner—on your favorite bun, in a lettuce wrap, or tossed in a salad. This Asian-inspired version, full of ginger, scallions, and garlic is super flavorful. But can we take a moment to chat about the spicy coconut peanut sauce? Once you take your first bite of these burgers, you will know exactly what I mean.

SERVES 4

Spicy Coconut Peanut Sauce

¼ cup crunchy or creamy **peanut butter**

3 tablespoons **full-fat coconut milk**

1 teaspoon **toasted sesame oil**

¼ teaspoon **sea salt**

2 tablespoons **coconut aminos**

1 tablespoon **Sriracha** sauce

Turkey Burgers

1 pound ground antibiotic- and hormone-free **turkey**

½ cup cooked **quinoa**

2 tablespoons chopped **scallions** (green parts only)

1 tablespoon **coconut aminos**

2 **garlic cloves**, minced

1 teaspoon **ground ginger**

½ teaspoon **sea salt**

1 teaspoon **freshly ground black pepper**

2 teaspoons **toasted sesame oil**

4 **gluten-free buns** or **lettuce wraps**

1. **Make the peanut sauce:** In a small bowl, whisk together the peanut butter, coconut milk, sesame oil, salt, coconut aminos, and Sriracha until fully combined. Set aside until ready to serve.

2. **Make the burgers:** In a large bowl, use a fork to mix the ground turkey, quinoa, scallions, coconut aminos, garlic, ginger, salt, and pepper until combined.

3. Divide the meat into 4 portions, and using your hands, form them into 1-inch-thick patties.

4. Heat the sesame oil in a large skillet over medium heat. Add the patties to the skillet, and press your thumb in the center of each one to form an indentation (this will help the burgers hold their shape as they cook).

5. Cook until the burgers are browned on the outside and completely cooked through, 5 to 7 minutes on each side.

6. Serve the warm burgers on buns or in lettuce wraps (or even in a bowl with your favorite mix-ins) with your desired toppings. Spoon the spicy coconut peanut sauce on top and enjoy. Leftover cooked burgers will keep in an airtight container in the fridge for up to 5 days.

Topping Ideas
Sliced avocado
Leafy greens
Sliced onion

Not into turkey? Sub in ground chicken or lamb. Both taste amazing in this recipe.

Wondering what to serve with these? Crispy Japanese Sweet Potato Fries (page 165) are perfection with the burgers!

bone broth–**poached chicken**

Poached chicken is my latest obsession when for those times when I want some tender and juicy chicken without roasting a whole bird. Bone broth is a staple in my daily life, whether I'm drinking a mugful or cooking with it. It is amazing for the gut, and packed with collagen and protein. You can cook with it as you would regular broth. By poaching chicken in broth instead of water, you add extra flavor to the chicken. It's such a simple, easy recipe to prep chicken breasts or tenders for the week.

SERVES 3 OR 4

1 medium **onion**, sliced

2 large **carrots**, sliced

2 large **celery stalks**, sliced

½ teaspoon **sea salt**

1 pound pasture-raised boneless, skinless **chicken breasts**

2 cups **chicken bone broth**

1. Add the onion, carrots, celery, salt, and chicken breasts to a large pot.

2. Pour in the bone broth and heat over medium heat until just before the broth begins to boil.

3. Reduce the heat to low, cover the pot, and simmer until a meat thermometer inserted in the thickest part of a breast registers 165°F, 20 to 25 minutes.

4. Transfer the chicken to a cutting board and discard the vegetables and poaching liquid. Shred the meat with two forks, slice it, or leave it whole for later use. The chicken will keep in an airtight container in the fridge for up to 5 days.

Wondering how to use this chicken? Stuff it into Veggie-Loaded Sheet Pan Fajitas (page 218), mix it into Creamy Alfredo Zucchini Noodles (page 209), or top your Sweet Potato Chip Nachos with it (page 109).

mini lamb meatballs
with tzatziki-tahini dipping sauce

Who here likes lamb? I tried lamb for the first time when I was twenty-seven and have been craving it daily ever since. Lamb has so much flavor on its own, and ground lamb makes for the best burgers and meatballs. The creamy coolness of a tzatziki-type sauce is a perfect partner to lamb, and this version adds the nutty accent of tahini. Enjoy these meatballs over a bed of quinoa or fresh greens in warmed pita breads for an at-home gyro! Not into lamb? Use your favorite ground meat: grass-fed beef, chicken, pork, etc.

SERVES 4

Mini Lamb Meatballs

1 pound ground
grass-fed **lamb**

1 large pasture-raised **egg**

⅓ cup **grain-free bread crumbs** (see page 29)

2 **garlic cloves**, minced

1 teaspoon **freshly ground black pepper**

½ teaspoon **sea salt**

Tzatziki-Tahini Dipping Sauce

½ cup **tahini**

⅓ cup **unsweetened nondairy yogurt**

Juice of ½ **lemon**

⅓ cup chopped **fresh dill**

½ teaspoon **sea salt**

½ cup chopped **English cucumber**

1. **Make the meatballs:** In a large bowl, use a fork or your hands to mix the ground lamb, egg, bread crumbs, garlic, pepper, and salt until combined.

2. Roll 1 to 2 tablespoons of the lamb mixture at a time into mini meatballs.

3. Heat a large skillet over medium heat. Add the meatballs to the hot skillet (you won't need oil for the skillet as the lamb is fatty). Cook for about 6 minutes, turn them, and cook until browned on all sides and cooked through, 6 to 8 minutes more. Transfer the meatballs to a paper towel-lined plate to drain.

4. **While the meatballs cook, make the tzatziki-tahini sauce:** In a medium bowl, combine the tahini, nondairy yogurt, 2 tablespoons of water, the lemon juice, dill, salt, and cucumber. Set aside.

5. Enjoy the meatballs with the tzatziki. Leftover cooked meatballs will keep in an airtight container in the fridge for about 5 days.

Pro Tip: Add some crumbled feta to the lamb meatballs when you are forming them. Such an insane flavor addition!

cracker-crusted oven-baked
fried chicken

Yeah baby, you can eat fried chicken now without feeling that you are overindulging. Instead of dipping the chicken thighs in bread crumbs and frying them in heavy oil, we're using gluten-free crackers for the coating and baking the chicken in the oven. This "fried" chicken is super simple to whip up and hits the spot when you want to switch up the usual chicken recipe rotation. Wondering what to serve with this? Warm Apple-Brussels Sprouts Slaw with Coconut Bacon (page 150) and Japanese Sweet Potato Fries (page 166) are awesome choices with some dreamy Dijon mustard—hot dayum!

SERVES 4

Avocado oil

4 boneless, skinless pasture-raised **chicken thighs**

2 large pasture-raised **eggs**

1 cup crushed **grain-free crackers** (should be similar to the consistency of panko)

1 teaspoon **smoked paprika**

2 teaspoons **garlic powder**

½ teaspoon **cayenne pepper**

1 teaspoon **freshly ground black pepper**

½ teaspoon **sea salt**

1. Preheat the oven to 425°F, line a baking sheet with parchment paper, and lightly grease the paper with avocado oil.

2. Pat the chicken thighs dry with paper towels.

3. Whisk the eggs in a shallow bowl.

4. In another shallow bowl, mix together the crushed crackers, paprika, garlic powder, cayenne, black pepper, and salt.

5. Dip each chicken thigh in the eggs, then in the crushed crackers, then back into the eggs and into the crushed crackers again.

6. Place the chicken thighs on the prepared baking sheet and bake for about 20 minutes, flipping them halfway through, until a meat thermometer inserted in the thickest part of a thigh reaches 165°F. Serve warm. This chicken recipe tastes best the day-of; I don't recommend making it in advance.

Want to switch up the crackers? Crushed gluten-free tortilla chips are a delicious option (for paleo, use cassava chips).

crispy maple-glazed
chicken wings

These wings will be your go-to for the next Super Bowl, game night, or whenever the wing craving strikes. The traditional spicy chicken wings from the place around the corner are officially replaced with this delicious savory-sticky-sweet version. Oven-baked and ready in under 30 minutes, they'll seriously be faster than any restaurant delivery option. Every time I sprinkle sesame seeds on top of them, I feel fancier than ever.

SERVES 4

3 tablespoons **gluten-free tapioca flour**

1 pound **pasture-raised chicken wings**

1 teaspoon **freshly ground black pepper**

¾ cup **coconut aminos**

2 tablespoons **coconut sugar**

¼ cup **pure maple syrup**

Sesame seeds, for garnish

1. Preheat the oven to 425°F and line a baking sheet with parchment paper.

2. Sprinkle the tapioca flour onto a large plate or shallow bowl. Roll the chicken wings in the flour until they are well coated. Transfer them to the prepared baking sheet.

3. Bake the chicken wings for 15 minutes, then flip and bake until they are crispy, about 15 minutes more.

4. While the chicken bakes, combine the pepper, coconut aminos, coconut sugar, and maple syrup in a small saucepan and whisk over medium-low heat until fully combined. Remove the pan from the heat.

5. When the chicken wings are done, transfer them to a large bowl, add the sauce, and toss until the wings are well coated.

6. Serve the wings warm with the sesame seeds sprinkled on top. The wings taste best the day they are made.

bison burger in a collard green wrap with avocado cream

Every time I talk about my love for bison, I feel like giggling. Bison meat sounds somewhat funny and random, but it is so underrated. The meat is a grainier and more flavorful version of beef, plus it's super satisfying and filling. Bison is my go-to at our local burger place, where I usually order it in a collard green wrap with some pickled onions and avocado. This is my take on that neighborhood fave, and I have to say the avocado cream kicks it to another level!

SERVES 4

4 large fresh **collard leaves**

1 pound ground grass-fed **bison** (buffalo)

1 teaspoon **freshly ground black pepper**

½ teaspoon **sea salt**

1 tablespoon **avocado oil**

Avocado Cream (recipe follows)

Topping Ideas

Lacto-fermented onions

Sliced lacto-fermented cucumbers

Sliced tomato

Sliced avocado

1. Using a paring knife, shave down the stems from the center of the collard leaves. This will make it easier to use the leaves as a wrap.

2. In a large bowl, mix together the ground bison, pepper, and salt. Using your hands, form the bison mixture into 4 equal patties.

3. Heat the oil in a large skillet over medium heat.

4. Add the patties to the hot skillet. Cook for 3 to 4 minutes on each side for rare or medium-rare (bison tends to get tough if cooked for too long). Remove the burgers from the skillet and allow them to rest on a plate for 10 to 15 minutes.

5. Place a burger on the center of a collard green and add your desired toppings. Fold one end of the leaf over the burger and continue wrapping the burger until it is completely encased in the leaf. Repeat with the remaining burgers. Slice the wrapped burgers in half.

6. Serve the burgers warm, with the avocado cream for dipping. Leftover cooked burgers can be stored in an airtight container in the fridge for up to 5 days and can be reheated in a greased skillet. Keep the collard greens, burgers, and toppings separate and assemble them just before serving.

avocado cream

MAKES 1 CUP

1 medium **avocado**, pitted and peeled

⅓ cup **avocado oil mayonnaise**

½ teaspoon chopped **garlic**

2 tablespoons chopped **fresh cilantro**

1. In a mini food processor or blender, combine the avocado, mayonnaise, garlic, and cilantro and blend until creamy.

2. Transfer the mixture to a small bowl and set it aside until ready to serve.

bacon + beef **meatballs**

Thanks to the additions of chopped bacon and crushed tortilla chips, these are the best meatballs I have ever eaten. (I cannot take full credit as it was totally Jord's idea.) Whenever someone tastes them for the first time, they can't pinpoint the secret ingredients. These meatballs are my go-to when we cook beef—they are amazing alongside veggies, added to your favorite spiralized veggie noodles, or on top of pasta! Did I mention meatball subs with these? They are a must-make. Not craving beef? You can sub any ground meat you'd like. Pork, turkey, and chicken all work in this recipe.

SERVES 4

1 tablespoon **avocado oil**

⅓ medium **white onion,** chopped

1 pound ground **grass-fed beef**

4 slices **nitrate-free, sugar-free bacon,** cooked and chopped

1 large pasture-raised **egg**

½ cup finely crushed **grain-free tortilla chips** (should be similar to the consistency of panko)

1 teaspoon **garlic powder**

½ teaspoon **cayenne pepper**

1 teaspoon **Italian seasoning**

½ teaspoon **freshly ground black pepper**

½ teaspoon **sea salt**

1. In a large skillet over medium heat, heat the avocado oil. Add the onion and sauté until softened, 5 to 7 minutes.

2. Transfer the onion to a large bowl (set the skillet aside) and add the ground beef, bacon, egg, crushed tortilla chips, garlic powder, cayenne, Italian seasoning, black pepper, and salt and mix well to combine.

3. Return the skillet to the stove and warm it over medium heat while you make the meatballs. With your hands, form 12 to 14 meatballs, using about 2 tablespoons of the mixture for each one.

4. Add the meatballs to the skillet and cook, turning them frequently, until they are browned on all sides, 12 to 15 minutes.

5. Transfer the meatballs to a paper towel-lined plate to drain before serving. Leftover cooked meatballs will keep in an airtight container in the fridge for up to 5 days, or in the freezer for up to 2 months.

zesty **jalapeño meatloaf**

True story: Meatloaf is likely the most unfortunate-looking dish to photograph. There isn't enough love for it out there in the food-blogging space, and I'm convinced that's because it is the most unattractive food. Sorry, meatloaf, ya ain't pretty, but you sure are tasty! This simple recipe spices up your traditional loaf and is that dreamy Sunday supper to serve when you want something comforting and nourishing for the soul. Plus, you'll have leftovers to enjoy all week long! Wondering what to serve with this? Besides roasted veggies, Chili Mac + Cheese (page 123) is a dream with this meatloaf.

SERVES 6

2 tablespoons **avocado oil**, plus more for greasing the loaf pan

1 small **onion**, chopped

2 **garlic cloves**, minced

2 pounds ground **grass-fed beef**

2 large pasture-raised **eggs**

⅓ cup blanched **almond flour**

⅓ cup plus 3 tablespoons **jalapeño ketchup** or **regular ketchup** (paleo, if preferred)

1 teaspoon **Italian seasoning**

½ teaspoon **freshly ground black pepper**

½ teaspoon **sea salt**

¼ cup chopped **jalapeños**

1. Preheat the oven to 375°F and grease a 9 × 5-inch loaf pan with avocado oil.

2. Add the avocado oil to a small skillet set over medium heat. Add the onion and garlic and sauté until softened, 5 to 7 minutes. Remove the skillet from the heat.

3. Transfer the garlic and onion to a large bowl and add the ground beef, eggs, almond flour, and 3 tablespoons of ketchup. Sprinkle with the Italian seasoning, pepper, and salt. Mix with your hands or with a fork until well combined.

4. Gently fold in the chopped jalapeños.

5. Transfer the meat mixture to the prepared loaf pan and bake for 25 minutes. Remove the pan from the oven, spread the remaining ⅓ cup ketchup over the top, and bake until the meatloaf is cooked through, 30 to 40 minutes more.

6. Let the meatloaf cool in the pan for a few minutes. Slice and serve. Leftovers will keep in an airtight container in the fridge for up to 5 days, or in the freezer for up to 2 months.

coconut flour–crusted
chicken tenders

Who else ordered chicken fingers at their college campus dining hall after a night out? I used to get something called a "chicken finger melt," which is basically a grilled cheese sandwich with two fried chicken fingers in the center. Yes, it was as over-the-top as it sounds, but it sure was delicious. These homemade chicken "fingers" were the first thing I ate when I reintroduced meat into my life a couple of years ago—and once you try them, you'll understand why! I love to serve these with Japanese Sweet Potato Latkes (page 120) or on top of the Garlicky Kale Caesar Salad (page 157).

SERVES 4 OR 5

3 large pasture-raised **eggs**

½ cup **coconut flour**

½ cup **gluten-free tapioca flour**

1 teaspoon **smoked paprika**

1 teaspoon **garlic powder**

½ teaspoon **sea salt**

2 pounds pasture-raised **chicken tenders** (or breasts, cut into strips)

2 tablespoons **avocado oil**, plus more as needed

1. In a shallow bowl, whisk the eggs.

2. In another shallow bowl, mix together the coconut flour, tapioca flour, paprika, garlic powder, and salt.

3. Dip each chicken tender into the eggs, then into the flour mixture, then again into the eggs and again into the flour mixture. Set on a large plate.

4. In a large skillet, heat the avocado oil over medium heat.

5. Add the breaded chicken tenders to the hot skillet and cook for about 3 minutes on each side, adding more avocado oil as needed, until golden brown and cooked through.

6. Serve warm with your desired dipping sauces.

vegetables

Oh, So Kale Can Actually Taste Good? The Tastiest Ways to Sneak in Those Veggies

Contrary to what one might think, vegetables and I didn't always get along. In fact, we still are working on our relationship. I'm not someone who craves veggies all the time and eats carrots or peppers as a snack. Growing up, I wanted to eat pretty much anything that was processed, loaded with sugar, and lathered with corn syrup. Pop-Tarts, Nutter Butter cookies, and Chewy Chips Ahoy cookies were just a few of my favorite snacks. (Oh, and don't forget Fruit Roll-Ups and Gushers.) I'd have a few apples and bananas here and there, but veggies definitely weren't my thing. In fact, I don't think I ate any type of vegetable besides fast-food French fries and onion rings. (Crazy, huh?)

I guess you can say that my taste buds evolved over time. After I went through a difficult phase (I weighed about twenty-five pounds less than I do today), I wanted to learn more about the best food for my body. I knew that if I was going to gain weight, feel good physically, and just have overall energy for life, Oreos weren't the way to do it. Yes, they taste really good from time to time (especially with peanut butter), but is that what I wanted to fuel my body with? I was thinking no.

I began reading about organic versus non-organic food, wild fish versus farmed, and so on. I started paying attention to the colors and types of food on my plate rather than the calories in it. As my perspective began to evolve, I focused more on the quality of the food I was eating. This was a major change for me because I was so used to counting calories and keeping under a certain fat threshold.

I started to find new and delicious ways to dress up vegetables and sneak them into things like breads and desserts (like the White Chocolate Carrot Cake Truffles on page 257). I finally started to appreciate veggies and wanted to include them on my plate when I could. I learned how to chop an onion, slice a pepper, and all different ways of preparing veg—roasting, steaming, sautéing, you name it. I realized that vegetables didn't need to be boring. I added coconut flakes to my sweet potatoes (see page 153), sweetened up my Brussels sprouts with warmed apples in a slaw (see page 150), and added spices to my roasted vegetables to make them as flavorful as possible.

I am sharing all my simple, tasty vegetable recipes with you in this chapter. Many of these recipes are my go-tos for food prepping for the week as well. I totally get it if vegetables aren't your thing, so ease into them. I'd be lying if I said I ate them at every meal, but I certainly try to incorporate them when I can!

> I totally get it if vegetables aren't your thing, so ease into them

warm apple–brussels sprout slac with coconut bacon

Brussels sprouts are a weekly staple for us during the winter. They can be pretty harsh on my stomach when I eat them raw, so I am always looking for new ways to cook them. We especially love roasting them for food prep (see page 37), but they are also delicious cooked in the skillet for this warm slaw. I love the sweet-tart combo and the crunchy coconut bacon mixed in—it adds the best texture. Plus, if you have leftover coconut bacon, it tastes amazing in scrambled eggs the next day!

SERVES 3 OR 4

1 pound **Brussels sprouts** (about 3 cups)

1 large **Honeycrisp apple**

⅓ cup **unsweetened coconut flakes**

1 tablespoon **avocado oil**

1 tablespoon **pure maple syrup**

½ teaspoon **ground cinnamon**

1 tablespoon **apple cider vinegar**

1. Trim the Brussels sprouts and remove any brown leaves.

2. In a food processor fitted with a shredding disc, shred the Brussels sprouts into small pieces (if you do not have a food processor, simply thinly slice the sprouts).

3. Core the apple and dice it into small pieces.

4. In a large dry skillet, toast the coconut flakes over medium heat until they are golden brown, 5 to 8 minutes.

5. Add the Brussels sprouts, apple, avocado oil, maple syrup, cinnamon, and apple cider vinegar to the skillet and mix well. Cook until the slaw is warmed through, 5 to 7 minutes. Serve it warm or cold. Leftover slaw will keep in an airtight container in the fridge for up to 5 days.

coconut-crusted sweet potato fries with cinnamon cashew dip

The sweet potato fries trend is here to stay, my friends. If there is one vegetable you will stock up on after looking through this book, it's likely to be sweet potatoes. Here is one reason why: you will be eating these coconut-crusted fries as though they were candy! Sweet potatoes have a natural sweetness to them (hence the name) and we are making that flavor pop here. Served with a homemade cinnamon cashew dip that tastes like Cinnamon Toast Crunch, they're a unique sweet spin on the usual savory classic.

SERVES 3 OR 4

Fries

2 large **sweet potatoes,** scrubbed

2 tablespoons **liquid coconut oil**

¼ cup **unsweetened shredded coconut**

1 teaspoon **ground cinnamon**

½ teaspoon **ground nutmeg**

Cinnamon Cashew Dip

½ cup **raw cashews**

1 cup boiling **filtered water**

1 teaspoon **ground cinnamon**

2 tablespoons **unsweetened nondairy milk**

1. Make the sweet potato fries: Preheat the oven to 325°F and line a baking sheet with parchment paper.

2. Slice the sweet potatoes into thin strips, place them in a large bowl, and toss with the coconut oil.

3. Sprinkle the shredded coconut, cinnamon, and nutmeg over the sweet potatoes and toss until they are well coated. Transfer the sweet potatoes to the prepared baking sheet.

4. Bake for 20 minutes, then flip and bake until tender, about 5 minutes more.

5. While the fries bake, make the cinnamon cashew dip: Add the cashews to a medium heatproof bowl and pour the boiling water over them. Soak for 20 minutes.

6. Drain the cashews and transfer them to a food processor. Add the cinnamon and nondairy milk, and blend until creamy, scraping down the sides of the bowl as needed.

7. Transfer the dip to a small bowl and serve it with the fries. Any leftover fries and dip will keep in airtight containers in the fridge for up to 5 days.

spicy **cauliflower wings**

Craving something a little spicy and packed with nutrients? I gotchu covered with these spicy cauliflower wings. Made with a hot and savory sauce, these wings are a guaranteed crowd pleaser, vegan or not. Even Jord (the king of chicken wings) loves to eat them. If you'd like, at the end, you can crisp them up a bit in some hot oil in a cast-iron skillet to get them extra crunchy.

SERVES 2 OR 3

1½ tablespoons **avocado oil**

2 tablespoons **coconut aminos**

2 tablespoons **pure maple syrup**

1 tablespoon **coconut flour**

1 teaspoon **cayenne pepper**

½ teaspoon **smoked paprika**

½ teaspoon **garlic powder**

1 teaspoon **crushed red pepper flakes**

1 teaspoon **chili powder**

1 large head **cauliflower**

1. Preheat the oven to 400°F and line a baking sheet with parchment paper.

2. In a large bowl, stir together the avocado oil, coconut aminos, maple syrup, coconut flour, cayenne, paprika, garlic powder, red pepper flakes, and chili powder.

3. Core the cauliflower and cut it into small florets. Add the florets to the bowl and toss with the sauce until well coated.

4. Transfer the cauliflower florets to the prepared baking sheet and bake, flipping them every 15 minutes or so, until golden brown, about 40 minutes total. Serve warm. Leftover cauliflower wings will keep in an airtight container in the fridge for up to 5 days.

garlicky kale caesar salad
with homemade croutons

When you think of Caesar salad, you're likely imagining a fattening, unhealthy salad served at the restaurant around the corner. But not this one! This garlicky kale Caesar is made with a dressing of tahini and avocado oil, plus homemade gluten-free croutons that are to die for. It's filled with healthy fats and flavor, and is a delicious base for your favorite toppings and protein. Wondering what to serve with this? Mini Lamb Meatballs (page 133), Bone Broth–Poached Chicken (page 132), and Ginger-Scallion Turkey Burgers (page 130) are all delicious with this salad!

SERVES 3 OR 4

3 slices **gluten-free bread**, cut into small cubes

1 tablespoon **liquid coconut oil** or **avocado oil**

1 teaspoon **garlic powder**

1 teaspoon **sea salt**

1 large bunch **dinosaur kale**

2 tablespoons **avocado oil**

¼ cup **tahini**

2 teaspoons **fresh lemon juice**

2 **garlic cloves**, minced

½ teaspoon **freshly ground black pepper**

1. Preheat the oven to 425°F and line a baking sheet with parchment paper.

2. Toss the bread cubes in a large bowl with the oil, garlic powder, and ½ teaspoon of the salt. Transfer the cubes to the prepared baking sheet and bake, flipping them halfway through, until toasted, 13 to 15 minutes. Set aside.

3. Remove the thick stems from the kale and stack the leaves on top of one another. Roll the leaves into a tight cylinder and slice them into thin strips. Place the strips into a large bowl.

4. In a small bowl, mix the avocado oil, tahini, 2 tablespoons of water, lemon juice, garlic, pepper, and the remaining ½ teaspoon salt until well combined.

5. Add the croutons and dressing to the kale, toss well, and serve. Leftover salad will keep in an airtight container in the fridge for up 5 days. Add fresh kale or other greens as desired to absorb some of the excess dressing.

charred romaine + zesty avocado salad

My salad game was forever changed when I tried grilled romaine at a Brooklyn restaurant a few years ago. As someone who prefers to eat my vegetables cooked rather than raw, I put this right into the "favorites" category. You might not expect to love warmed lettuce, but the second you bite into this, your salads will rise to a new level. This is a deliciously simple salad that goes well with your favorite protein or on its own as a starter. Plus, it is very allergy friendly for most people (cilantro haters not included!). I char up my romaine in a skillet, but if you have a grill or a grill pan, go for it!

SERVES 2

1 large head **romaine lettuce**

2 tablespoons **avocado oil**

1 medium **avocado**

2 tablespoons chopped **fresh cilantro**

½ teaspoon **garlic powder**

½ teaspoon **sea salt**

½ teaspoon **freshly ground black pepper**

½ **lemon**

> Looking for something to serve this with? Those Coconut Flour–Crusted Chicken Tenders (page 147) are delicious with this salad and make for a satisfying, protein-filled meal!

1. Without separating the leaves, wash the romaine under cold water. Prop it base-up and let it dry for a few minutes.

2. Slice the romaine lengthwise into quarters, taking care to keep the base intact for each piece so the leaves stay connected.

3. In a large skillet, heat 1 tablespoon of the avocado oil over medium heat. Add the romaine and cook until it starts to soften and turn brown, about 4 minutes on each side. Remove from the heat.

4. Peel and pit the avocado and slice it into chunks. Place the avocado in a medium bowl and add the remaining tablespoon of avocado oil along with the cilantro, garlic powder, salt, and pepper. Mix well.

5. Divide the grilled romaine between two plates and top it with the avocado. Squeeze the lemon over the salad and serve immediately.

vegan animal-style **french fries**

Every time we go to California, Jord heads to In-N-Out Burger basically straight off the plane. I asked him once if he was going to get "animal-style" fries and he had zero idea what I was talking about. Guess that secret menu item is still secret to some! As a person who has eaten at In-N-Outs during many trips to California, I have had my fair share of animal-style fries—covered with cheese, mayo, ketchup, and caramelized onions. This recipe, a vegan, healthier spin on the original, uses jalapeño cashew cheese and a homemade "secret sauce" that will top off the most outstanding batch of french fries you have ever made in your kitchen!

SERVES 3 OR 4

Fries

3 medium **white potatoes**

1 tablespoon **avocado oil**

Sea salt and **freshly ground black pepper**

Secret Sauce

3 tablespoons **avocado oil mayonnaise**

2 tablespoons **sugar-free ketchup**

2 teaspoons **Dijon mustard**

1 teaspoon **pure maple syrup**

Sea salt and **freshly ground black pepper**

Toppings

Jalapeño Cashew "Cheese" (page 110)

½ cup Simple but Epic Caramelized Onions (page 162)

1. Preheat the oven to 425°F and line a baking sheet with parchment paper.

2. **Make the fries:** Cut the potatoes lengthwise into small, thin fries. In a medium bowl, toss the fries with the avocado oil to coat them. Season them lightly with salt and pepper. Transfer the fries to the prepared baking sheet and bake until they start to crisp and turn golden brown, 35 to 40 minutes.

3. **While the fries cook, make the secret sauce:** In a small bowl, combine the mayo, ketchup, Dijon mustard, and maple syrup, and season with salt and pepper to taste. Stir until smooth.

4. Once the fries are ready, transfer them to a serving plate and top them with the cashew cheese, caramelized onions, and secret sauce. Serve warm and fresh from the oven.

simple but epic
caramelized onions

When in doubt, add some caramelized onions to a dish. These tender, sweet onions make their way into pretty much everything at our house. Add them to scrambled eggs, put them in tacos, scatter them on top of pizza, and just eat them straight from the container while you cook dinner (I promise I am not a complete weirdo). Prepping them is so simple and requires minimal effort. Seriously, this is the easiest recipe in the book! Wondering what to serve these with? They are wonderful on pretty much any savory bowl, but I especially love them on top of the Spaghetti Squash Pizza Crust (page 188).

MAKES ABOUT 1 CUP

2 large **white onions**

1 tablespoon **avocado oil**

1. Slice the onions into thin rings.

2. In a large skillet, heat the avocado oil over medium heat. Add the onions and cook until they start to brown, about 5 minutes.

3. Reduce the heat to medium-low, cover the skillet, and cook the onions, stirring them occasionally, until they are well caramelized, 30 to 40 minutes.

4. Serve the onions warm. Store leftover caramelized onions in an airtight container in the fridge for up to 5 days and reheat in a greased skillet.

roasted turmeric
carrot fries

Rainbow carrots make this dish so gorgeous, filling it with beautiful oranges, yellows, and purples. The longer you roast them the better—I like mine very, very well done. I love that there is turmeric in this recipe—it doesn't have a strong flavor and you somehow forget about it until your hands turn a little orange when you start eating the fries straight from the pan (bound to happen). Turmeric is a great healthy and anti-inflammatory spice to sneak in whenever you can!

SERVES 3 OR 4

8 large rainbow **carrots**

2 tablespoons **avocado oil**

1 teaspoon **ground turmeric**

½ teaspoon **garlic powder**

½ teaspoon **dried thyme**

1. Preheat the oven to 425°F and line a baking sheet with parchment paper.

2. Slice the carrots in half crosswise, then lengthwise into ½-inch-thick pieces.

3. In a large bowl, toss together the carrots, avocado oil, turmeric, garlic powder, and thyme. Transfer the carrots to the prepared baking sheet.

4. Bake for 25 minutes, then flip and bake until they are tender and roasted to your liking, about 10 minutes more. Serve warm or at room temperature. Leftover carrot fries will keep in an airtight container in the fridge for up to 5 days.

my favorite crispy
japanese sweet potato fries

This is so simple, I almost feel guilty calling it a recipe. But I'd be doing you a disservice if I didn't include my absolute favorite sweet potato fries here. One of the most common questions I receive from my Instagram community is how to make them! My mom first introduced me to Japanese sweet potatoes when I was staying with my parents in Florida. Once I had one, I was shoveling them all into my mouth like a crazy person: "Oh my gosh, these are amazing! How have I never eaten these before?!" Japanese sweet potatoes get super crunchy, as you'll see (my secret technique is to begin to crisp them in a skillet first!) and have a subtle sweet flavor that I actually love even more than the familiar orange sweet potato. Well worth the hunt to find these at the grocery store!

SERVES 3 OR 4

2 large **Japanese sweet potatoes**, scrubbed

1 teaspoon **freshly ground black pepper**

½ teaspoon **sea salt**

1 tablespoon **avocado oil**

1. Preheat the oven to 425°F and line a baking sheet with parchment paper.

2. Cut the ends off the potatoes and slice the rounded edges off the sides. Slice each trimmed sweet potato in half lengthwise. Slice each half into strips about ½ inch thick and sprinkle them with the pepper and salt.

3. In a large skillet, heat the avocado oil over medium-high heat. Add the sweet potatoes and cook, flipping them halfway through, until they are lightly golden, 5 to 7 minutes. Transfer the fries to the prepared baking sheet.

4. Bake the fries for 25 minutes. Flip them and cook until they are golden brown and crispy, about 20 minutes more. Enjoy while warm. Leftover fries will keep in an airtight container in the fridge for up to 5 days.

Can't find organic Japanese sweet potatoes? Sub any other sweet potato you can find.

Food prepping these? I recommend letting them cool completely before storing in a glass container so they don't get soggy.

garlicky **oven-roasted mushrooms**

Mushrooms are the ugly duckling of the vegetable family and sadly underrated in my opinion. They're my favorite to add to pasta bowls or stuff in a quesadilla (see page 206). Cooking them in some avocado oil and garlic makes the mushrooms extra flavorful but doesn't overpower them. I make shiitakes most often, but any mushrooms will work!

SERVES 3 OR 4

2 cups **mushrooms** (such as button, shiitakes, or a mix)

2 tablespoons **avocado oil**

2 **garlic cloves**, minced

2 tablespoons chopped **scallions** (white and green parts)

1. Preheat the oven to 400°F and line a baking sheet with parchment paper.

2. Clean the mushrooms by wiping off any dirt with a damp paper towel. Remove and discard the stems. Slice the mushroom caps in half if they are very large.

3. In a large bowl, toss the mushrooms with the avocado oil, garlic, and scallions. Transfer them to the prepared baking sheet and roast until they are cooked through, 10 to 12 minutes. Serve while still warm. Leftovers will keep in an airtight container in the fridge for up to 5 days.

I recommend adding these to dinner bowls, on top of bison burgers (see page 140), and to the Waffled Veggie Burger Breakfast Sammie (page 210).

crispy **brussels sprouts**

Just putting it out there: roasting Brussels sprouts will definitely stink up your kitchen. I can just see my dad's face whenever he walks in when Brussels sprouts are in the oven. But they are so good and so worth the smell. Just blast your air purifier, crack open a window, burn some palo santo, and you are set. These sprouts are extra crispy and almost fried-like—I cannot get enough! Dipped right into Dijon mustard, they're too delicious. After giving birth, I was finally able to tolerate roasted Brussels sprouts again—that was the most random pregnancy aversion for the entire nine months!

SERVES 4

1 pound **Brussels sprouts** (about 3 cups)

2 tablespoons **avocado oil**

½ teaspoon **freshly ground black pepper**

½ teaspoon **garlic powder**

½ teaspoon **sea salt**

1. Preheat the oven to 425°F and line a baking sheet with parchment paper.

2. Trim the Brussels sprouts, removing any brown leaves. Slice them in half and place them in a large bowl. Add the avocado oil, pepper, garlic powder, and salt, and toss until they are well coated.

3. Transfer the Brussels sprouts to the prepared baking sheet and bake, flipping them halfway through (add more oil if they look dry), until they turn golden, about 30 minutes. Turn the broiler on high and crisp the sprouts for about 1 minute. Serve immediately. Leftover sprouts will keep in an airtight container in the fridge for up to 5 days. Reheat them in a skillet greased with a bit of avocado oil.

roasted **rainbow veggie slaw**

Vegetable slaws are typically consumed raw, but this colorful version—filled with potatoes, zucchini, carrots, and onions—is a warm cooked slaw that is amazing as a side dish with your dinner or brought to a friend's summer barbecue. (It's also delicious eaten cold out of the fridge after it's cooked.) Feel free to switch up the veggies however you please, as this will definitely be a regular in your kitchen once you try it!

MAKES 2 CUPS

1 large **white potato**, peeled

1 large **zucchini**

1 large **carrot**

1 large **white onion**

2 tablespoons **Dijon mustard**

1 tablespoon **avocado oil**

½ teaspoon **cayenne pepper**

½ teaspoon **garlic powder**

½ teaspoon **freshly ground black pepper**

½ teaspoon **sea salt**

1. Preheat the oven to 425°F and line a baking sheet with parchment paper.

2. Thinly slice the potato, zucchini, carrot, and onion, and then cut the slices into matchstick-like pieces.

3. Place the sliced vegetables in a large bowl and add the Dijon mustard, avocado oil, cayenne, garlic powder, black pepper, and salt. Mix until well coated.

4. Transfer the vegetables to the prepared baking sheet and bake, stirring every 15 minutes or so, until they start to turn golden, about 45 minutes total. Serve warm or chilled—either way tastes amazing! Leftover slaw will keep in an airtight container in the fridge for up to 5 days.

roasted **spaghetti squash**

When you pick up a spaghetti squash at the grocery store, you may likely scratch your head, wondering what to do with it and how to roast it. It is quite simple, though, and once you have made this comforting veggie, you will want it again and again. Use it as a great pasta sub, turn it into a pizza crust (see page 188), or for a lightened-up pasta dish, try topping the squash with the Bacon + Beef Meatballs (page 143) and some marinara sauce.

SERVES 2

1 large **spaghetti squash**

1 tablespoon **avocado oil**

1. Preheat the oven to 425°F and line a baking sheet with parchment paper.

2. Carefully slice the spaghetti squash in half lengthwise (if it's too tough to slice, microwave it for 1 minute or warm in the oven for 5 minutes to soften it). Scoop out the seeds in the center and discard them, or roast them for a snack (see Note).

3. Rub the avocado oil all over the interior of the squash. Place the squash halves, cut-side down, on the prepared baking sheet. Bake for 20 minutes, then flip and bake until they are tender when pierced with a sharp knife, about 20 minutes more.

4. Let the spaghetti squash cool for about 5 minutes. Using a fork, loosen the flesh so it separates into pasta-like threads. Scoop out the flesh and serve the spaghetti squash as you would any pasta. Leftover spaghetti squash will keep in an airtight container in the fridge for up to 5 days. Reheat in a greased skillet or in microwave.

Roasting the squash seeds? I season mine with some avocado oil, cinnamon, nutmeg, and cardamom for a sweet, crunchy snack. Roast them in the oven at 425°F until crispy, 15 to 20 minutes.

gatherings

Finding Your Tribe and Feeding Them Well

I feel so lucky to be surrounded by a supportive network of friends from all parts of my life. Some of my closest friends are people I've met through Instagram and blogging or at various events and functions in the wellness space. We have traveled all over the country together, visited each other's homes, talked on the phone weekly, and communicated daily via text and Instagram. I confide in these friends and have a strong bond with them. I have the most amazing blog readers and have connected with hundreds of them via email, messaging, events, and more. It is one of my favorite parts about what I do—being able to share similar vulnerabilities and pasts that bring us together on a level deeper than just both loving avocado toast.

Establishing new friendships is something I believe will continue as I get older. We discover more about who we are and begin relating to more people, meeting new friends from the local fitness studio, a favorite coffee shop, and—my personal favorite—through mutual friends. I have found that "my people" also thrive off finding a new organic dark chocolate or trying the new bone broth shop in town. These friendships have been so special—they've helped me grow as a person and feel less alone in my taste in food. They have also helped me become more confident: being surrounding by uplifting people has helped my relationship with myself. I have found my tribe, and I could not be more grateful for that!

When I started inviting friends over for dinner or for appetizers and drinks, I felt like I was #adulting in a way I hadn't before. *Cooking for other people? You mean, making a meal for more than just me and Jord? How do I cook for more than two people?* We have discovered that we love having others over for dinner and going to friends' potlucks and dinner parties—it is more intimate and can be more affordable than going out every weekend. After trying it, you'll see how much pride and joy you'll take in serving home-cooked dishes to friends and family. Pick a recipe (or two) from this chapter and invite a few friends over to enjoy it with you. Dinner parties and potlucks have never been easier.

> You'll soon see how much pride and joy you'll take in serving home-cooked dishes.

charred avocados stuffed
with crab salad

Fresh crab salad always reminds me of my mom because she used to make us crab cakes whenever my brother and I were home. These stuffed avocados are my favorite way to enjoy crab these days, and they're an easy fresh dish to kick off a dinner party or enjoy as a lighter meal. Charred avocados have an amazing flavor—I use my cast-iron skillet, but if you have a grill or a grill pan, even better!

SERVES 6 TO 8

12 ounces wild-caught **lump crabmeat**

3 tablespoons **avocado oil mayonnaise**

3 tablespoons chopped **scallions** (green parts only)

¼ cup chopped **celery**

½ teaspoon **freshly ground black pepper**

½ teaspoon **sea salt**

4 medium **avocados**

1 tablespoon **avocado oil**

1. Drain any excess liquid from the crabmeat and place it in a large bowl. Add the mayo, scallions, celery, pepper, and salt and stir until well combined.

2. Slice each avocado in half and remove the pit.

3. Heat a large cast-iron skillet over medium heat. Grease the skillet with the avocado oil. Add the avocados, cut-side down. Cook until browned, about 4 minutes. Flip and cook until the avocados are warmed through and browned on the second side, 4 to 5 minutes longer.

4. Remove the avocados from the skillet and fill the cavities with the crab salad. Serve immediately.

Don't have any crabmeat? Sub in fresh lobster meat as another delicious option.

cauliflower rice **sushi rolls**

I created this recipe when I had extra cauliflower rice in the freezer and zero idea what to do with it. (It was on sale at the grocery store and I had stocked up like a mad woman.) We had friends over for dinner and wanted to serve a fun finger food as an appetizer, and I came up with these beauties! If you have a bamboo sushi mat, then great. If not, just use some wax paper and go to town. Don't forget the chopsticks!

SERVES 4

1 (12- to 15-ounce) bag organic **cauliflower rice**, or 1 small head **cauliflower**

2 teaspoons **avocado oil**

2 tablespoons **coconut milk**

4 large sheets **nori**

½ cup thinly sliced **carrots**

½ cup thinly sliced **cucumber**

½ cup thinly sliced **avocado**

Coconut aminos, for dipping

Want to add some protein? Roll up some wild ahi tuna, salmon, or shrimp inside!

1. If you are using a head of cauliflower, core it, cut it into large pieces, and pulse them in a food processor until they are broken into small rice-like pieces. You should have 3 to 4 cups.

2. Heat the avocado oil in a large skillet over medium heat. Add the cauliflower rice and cook until it has softened a bit, 5 to 8 minutes.

3. Remove the skillet from the heat and stir in the coconut milk. Let the mixture cool for a few minutes, either at room temperature or in the fridge to speed up the process.

4. Lay the nori sheets on a bamboo mat or wax paper, cover them with a damp paper towel, and let them soften for a couple of minutes.

5. Gently press a quarter (about ¼ cup) of the cauliflower rice onto the lower two-thirds of a sheet of nori, leaving at least 1 inch empty at the top. Smush the cauliflower rice down a bit.

6. Arrange a handful of carrot, cucumber, and avocado in a line over the center of the cauliflower.

7. Starting from the bottom, gently roll the nori sheet up, folding it over the cauliflower and veggies, using the mat as a guide. Wet the top section of the nori sheet with water and continue rolling to seal the roll. Repeat with the remaining nori sheets and fillings.

8. Cut each roll into 6 equal rounds with a sharp knife. Serve with the coconut aminos for dipping.

slow-cooker
quinoa burrito bowls

Okay, I have to admit something. We didn't buy a slow cooker until last year. Meanwhile, all my friends were bragging about their chilis and soups and toasting bread in their slow cookers (okay, totally made that last one up). Jord and I just never had the desire to buy one until we found the space to store it in the kitchen. Slow cookers are not tiny, that's for sure! These burrito bowls have converted me to the slow-cooking life (and, especially as a mama, it streamlines my time in the kitchen). These bowls are packed with flavor and easy to make. You can wow your guests and they won't even know it took no time at all to whip this up!

SERVES 6

1 cup uncooked **quinoa**

1 cup **vegetable broth**

⅓ cup chunky **salsa**

1 teaspoon **chili powder**

1 teaspoon **smoked paprika**

½ teaspoon **garlic powder**

½ teaspoon **sea salt**

½ teaspoon **freshly ground black pepper**

2 tablespoons **nutritional yeast**

Medium **gluten-free tortillas**, warmed, or **tortilla chips**, for serving

Topping Ideas

Sliced avocado

Chopped fresh cilantro

Black beans

Corn kernels

Lime wedges

1. Place the quinoa in a fine-mesh sieve and rinse it under cool running water to remove its natural coating of saponins. Drain thoroughly.

2. Transfer the drained quinoa to a slow cooker and add the vegetable broth, salsa, chili powder, paprika, garlic powder, salt, pepper, and nutritional yeast. Stir to combine.

3. Cover and cook on the low setting until the quinoa is fully cooked, 2½ to 4 hours.

4. Serve the quinoa warm in bowls with the toppings of your choice, and with the tortillas or tortilla chips alongside.

Having some friends over for dinner? This is an easy no-fuss recipe that requires minimal prep work and is perfect for most dietary preferences.

Don't have a slow cooker? Cook the quinoa with the broth in a saucepan according to the package instructions. Mix in the salsa and spices and serve as described.

carrot-zucchini noodles
with almond butter sauce

Carrot and zucchini noods—"so hot right now," as Jord would say. There isn't anything a spiralized veggie can't do, and these carrots and zucchini are the best base for this nutty noodle dish. The addictive almond butter sauce has no soy or added sugar. Soba noodles would go amazingly well in this dish—just add them in with the veggies. This is definitely a meal that is delicious hot or cold, making it perfect to bring to a potluck or picnic.

SERVES 4 TO 6

Almond Butter Sauce

⅓ cup **creamy almond butter**

⅔ cup **chicken or vegetable broth**

2 tablespoons **toasted sesame oil**

⅓ cup **coconut aminos**

3 tablespoons **apple cider vinegar**

2 tablespoons **coconut flour**

2 **garlic cloves**, minced

Noodles

5 large **zucchini** (if buying prepared zoodles, you'll need 5 to 7 cups)

3 large **carrots** (if buying prepared spiralized carrots, you'll need 3 to 4 cups)

2 tablespoons **avocado oil**

1 **red bell pepper**, chopped

1 **orange bell pepper**, chopped

1 **white onion**, chopped

1. **Make the almond butter sauce:** In a medium saucepan, stir together the almond butter, chicken broth, sesame oil, coconut aminos, apple cider vinegar, coconut flour, and garlic. Warm the sauce over medium heat until it starts to thicken, about 2 minutes. Reduce the heat to low, cover the pan, and keep on a low simmer until ready to use.

2. **Make the noodles:** Using a spiralizer, turn the zucchini and carrots into noodles.

3. Warm the avocado oil in a large skillet over medium heat. Add the zucchini, carrots, bell peppers, and onion and cook, stirring frequently, until softened, 8 to 10 minutes.

4. Pour the almond butter sauce over the vegetables and toss to coat. Serve warm, with your choice of toppings. Leftovers will keep in an airtight container in the fridge for up to 5 days. Reheat them in a skillet over medium-low heat until warmed through.

Topping Ideas

Scrambled pasture-raised eggs

Chopped scallions (white
and green parts)

Chopped fresh cilantro

Sliced avocado

Protein of choice

Chopped nuts

Sesame seeds

Taco Topping Ideas

Leafy greens

Lacto-fermented pickled onions

Chunky salsa

Fresh cilantro leaves

Extra protein (the Bone Broth–Poached Chicken on page 132 is a great option!)

crispy avocado tacos
with herbed cashew cheese

This herbed cashew cheese has quickly found its way into my weekly lineup. I used to buy nut cheeses at the grocery store, and still do from time to time, but nothing beats making your own preservatives-free batch!

SERVES 6

Herbed Cashew Cheese

1 cup **raw cashews**

1½ cups boiling **filtered water**

¼ cup chopped **scallions** (green parts only)

½ teaspoon **garlic powder**

½ teaspoon **sea salt**

½ teaspoon **freshly ground black pepper**

2 tablespoons **nutritional yeast**

2 tablespoons **unsweetened nondairy milk**

4 medium **avocados**

⅔ cup **grain-free bread crumbs**

¼ cup **gluten-free tapioca flour**

2 teaspoons **smoked paprika**

1 teaspoon **garlic powder**

½ teaspoon **sea salt**

½ teaspoon **freshly ground black pepper**

¼ cup **avocado oil**, plus more

6 medium **grain-free tortillas**

1. **Make the cashew cheese:** Add the cashews to a medium heatproof bowl and cover them with the boiling water. Soak the cashews for 20 minutes, then drain.

2. Transfer the drained cashews to a food processor and add the scallions, garlic powder, salt, pepper, nutritional yeast, and nondairy milk and blend until a thick, creamy paste forms, scraping down the sides of the bowl as necessary. Use immediately or store in an airtight container in the refrigerator for up to 5 days.

3. Cut each avocado in half and remove the pit and skin. Slice the halves into thick slices, 6 to 8 slices per avocado.

4. In a medium shallow bowl, mix together the bread crumbs, tapioca flour, paprika, garlic powder, salt, and pepper. Pour the avocado oil into a small shallow bowl.

5. Dip each slice of avocado in the bowl of oil, and then dredge it in the bread crumb mixture.

6. Heat a large skillet over medium heat and add a generous amount of avocado oil. Cook the avocado slices in the hot oil until each side is golden brown and crispy, 3 to 5 minutes per side.

7. Divide the fried avocados among the warmed tortillas, and add the cashew cheese and your choice of toppings.

spaghetti squash **pizza crust**

I love slipping veggies into recipes where you'd least expect to see them. There was a time that cauliflower pizza crust was the be-all and end-all of alt-pizza crusts. I made it often and enjoyed it, but then cauliflower turned up in my smoothies, in my fried rice, and next thing I knew, I saw it in a baking mix. I was starting to get a bit tired of cauliflower so often, so hello, spaghetti squash! This crust is so simple to make, you'll be wondering why you haven't been cooking it this way forever. Of course, it doesn't satisfy cravings for *real* pizza (nothing does, in my opinion), but it sure is delicious and the topping possibilities are endless! I love making it for an appetizer when friends are coming over and we want to nosh on something healthy before dinner. Or you can serve it as the main event—just double the ingredients and make two pies!

MAKES 1 SMALL PIZZA

Roasted Spaghetti Squash
(page 174)

1 **flax egg** (see page 29)

½ teaspoon **chili powder**

¼ teaspoon **garlic powder**

¼ teaspoon **dried oregano**

Topping Ideas
Herbed Cashew Cheese
(page 187)

Fresh basil leaves

Marinara sauce

Grated cheese (both dairy and nondairy are great here)

Cooked chicken sausage or vegan sausage, sliced

Roasted vegetables, sliced

1. Preheat the oven to 425°F and line a baking sheet with parchment paper.

2. In a large bowl, mix together the squash, flax egg, chili powder, garlic powder, and oregano.

3. On the prepared baking sheet, form the squash mixture into a pizza of your desired shape, about 1 inch thick.

4. Bake the crust just until it starts to turn golden, about 30 minutes. Remove it from the oven, add your desired toppings, and return it to the oven. Cook until the edges are golden brown, 10 to 15 minutes more. Slice and serve warm. Leftover pizza will keep in an airtight container in the fridge for up to 5 days. Reheat it in the oven at 350°F.

thai coconut squash soup

This squash soup is so creamy (yet has no cream) and has an extra zing from the red curry paste. I know it can be annoying to have to buy an ingredient just for one recipe, but the curry paste comes in a small container and lasts a long time in the fridge. This soup is a great light meal, or you can add some protein (like the chicken on page 132) to make it more filling.

SERVES 5 OR 6

4 cups 1-inch cubed and peeled **butternut squash**

4 tablespoons **avocado oil**

Sea salt and **freshly ground black pepper**

4 cups **filtered water**

3 cups **full-fat coconut milk**

2 teaspoons finely chopped **fresh ginger**

8 teaspoons **red curry paste**

½ cup **unsweetened coconut flakes**, toasted

Fresh **basil leaves** (optional)

Sriracha sauce (optional)

1. Preheat the oven to 425°F and line two baking sheets with parchment paper.

2. Spread the cubes of butternut squash on the prepared baking sheets. Drizzle them with 2 tablespoons of the avocado oil and season lightly with salt and pepper. Roast until they are tender enough to cut with a fork, 30 to 40 minutes.

3. Allow the squash cubes to cool for about 5 minutes. Put them in a blender, pour in the filtered water, and blend until creamy, about 2 to 3 minutes.

4. Pour the squash puree into a large pot set over medium heat. Add the remaining 2 tablespoons avocado oil and the coconut milk, ginger, and red curry paste. (If the soup is too thick, add more water or coconut milk, ¼ cup at a time, stirring thoroughly after each addition, to thin it out.) Season the soup with salt and pepper.

5. Cook until the soup is heated through, about 15 minutes. Serve the warm soup in bowls, with the toasted coconut flakes scattered on top. Garnish with the basil leaves and Sriracha, if using. Any leftover soup (hold the coconut flakes) will keep in an airtight container in the fridge for up to 5 days, or in the freezer for a couple of months.

greek salad pinwheels

When I was younger, pinwheels were my jam! I knew we were having guests over when my mom was rolling these up, and I would always hope there'd be some leftovers. Stuffed with hummus, feta, olives, and veggies, these bites are flavorful and delicious. I was never much of a wrap girl at the local deli, but I am all about these pinwheel beauties. They are addictive and such a fun finger food to serve.

MAKES ABOUT 16 PINWHEELS

2 large **gluten-free tortillas**

½ cup sprouted **hummus**

¼ cup crumbled
sheep's-milk feta

¼ cup chopped **tomato**

¼ cup chopped pitted
kalamata olives

1½ cups fresh **baby spinach**

1. Lay the tortillas out on a cutting board. Spread the hummus evenly over each one. Divide the feta, tomato, olives, and spinach between the tortillas, covering the tortillas completely.

2. Use your hands to flatten the fillings, and then tightly roll up the tortillas. Place them seam-side down on the cutting board or on a plate.

3. Chill the rolls in the fridge for 30 minutes or up to 2 hours (you can wrap them in plastic wrap or leave them uncovered).

4. Remove the wraps from the fridge and cut each roll into about 8 pieces.

5. Arrange the pinwheels on a large plate and serve.

crunchy veggie soba noodle rolls with spicy nutty sauce

Inspired by one of my fave vegan sushi spots in Manhattan, these rolls are stuffed with crunchy vegetables, creamy avocado, and slippery soba noodles. The best part: they're dipped in an addictive nutty sauce. They are insanely good. Not gonna lie, they're a bit time consuming since you do have to roll each one individually, but once you get the hang of it, you're set. The rolls are a fun appetizer to serve at a dinner party and are also one of my go-to lunch options.

SERVES 5 OR 6

Spicy Nutty Sauce

½ cup **creamy nut butter**

2 tablespoons **coconut aminos**

2 tablespoons **pure maple syrup**

1 tablespoon **fresh lime juice**

2 teaspoons **toasted sesame oil**

¼ cup hot **filtered water**

½ teaspoon **crushed red pepper flakes**

Summer Rolls

Hot **filtered water**, for soaking

10 **rice paper wraps**

1 cup cooked **soba noodles** or brown rice noodles

1 cup **leafy greens**

1 cup thinly sliced **carrots**

1 cup thinly sliced **cucumber**s

⅓ cup unsalted **raw peanuts** or almonds

2 medium **avocados**, sliced

¼ cup chopped **fresh cilantro**

1. **Make the sauce:** In a small pot, combine the nut butter, coconut aminos, maple syrup, lime juice, sesame oil, hot water, and red pepper flakes. Warm over medium heat, stirring frequently, until the sauce is combined. Remove the pot from the heat and set it aside.

2. **Make the rolls:** Fill a shallow bowl about halfway with hot water

3. Completely submerge a rice paper wrap in the hot water for about 15 seconds and transfer it to a damp cutting board.

4. Place a small handful of soba noodles in the center of the rice paper wrap, followed by some of the leafy greens, carrots, cucumbers, peanuts, avocado, and cilantro.

5. Fold the bottom half of the wrap up over the filling, tuck in the sides, and then roll it up tightly to form a summer roll. Repeat with the remaining wraps and fillings. Set the rolls aside until ready to serve, covering them with a damp paper towel so they don't dry out. (I leave them at room temperature if I am eating within the hour; otherwise I put them in the fridge.)

6. Serve the rolls with the sauce alongside for dipping. These rolls will keep in an airtight container in the fridge for up to 5 days, but the avocado may brown a bit. Scoop it out or omit if you are making them in advance.

oven-baked **salmon burgers**

There is no such thing as too many salmon burgers at our place. I am always trying out new recipes, and seriously, this is the best salmon burger I've created yet. They are made with just five ingredients (not counting the salt and pepper), and because they bake in the oven they won't smell up your kitchen (sorry, salmon, but it happens). Prepare them when you're having friends over for dinner and serve some Crispy Japanese Sweet Potato Fries (page 166) alongside for a comforting, hearty, and healthy get-together!

SERVES 8

2 (15-ounce) cans **wild salmon**, drained

⅔ cup blanched **almond flour**

½ teaspoon **sea salt**

1 teaspoon **freshly ground black pepper**

2 large pasture-raised **eggs**

⅓ cup chopped **scallions** (green parts only)

¼ cup **avocado oil mayonnaise**

8 large **lettuce leaves** (for wraps) or **gluten-free hamburger buns** or **English muffins**

Topping Ideas

Sliced avocado

Leafy greens

Spicy mayo (Sriracha mixed with any mayo!)

Pickled onions

Sheep's-milk feta, goat cheese, or nondairy cheese

Sweet Potato Fries (page 166), for serving

1. Preheat the oven to 375°F and line a 9 × 13-inch baking dish with parchment paper.

2. In a large bowl, mix together the salmon, almond flour, salt, pepper, eggs, scallions, and mayonnaise. Using your hands or a ½-cup measuring cup, form the mixture into 8 patties.

3. Place the patties in the prepared baking dish and bake for 10 minutes. Flip and bake until cooked through, about 10 minutes more.

4. Top and serve them as you like and enjoy them with the sweet potato fries. Freeze any extra cooked burgers in an airtight container for up to 2 months, and reheat them when you're ready to eat.

Can't eat nuts?
Sub ¼ cup oat flour or sprouted spelt flour for the almond flour.

Making this recipe for only a few people? Feel free to cut the ingredient amounts in half to make four burgers.

my mama liss's **enchilada pie**

Jord and I have been together since I was nineteen years old. We got married when I was twenty-five, but a couple of years prior, I actually lived with my in-laws-to-be when I was commuting into the city. My mother-in-law opened up her kitchen to me and taught me the ins and outs of how to make delicious, simple, real food. I didn't even know how to cook a piece of chicken or slice an onion! This creative enchilada pie is one of Elissa's signature dishes—it's always a hit and I think you'll see why.

SERVES 4

Avocado oil, for greasing the baking dish

3 large (9-inch) **grain-free tortillas**

1 cup **shredded chicken** (I love the Bone Broth–Poached Chicken on page 132)

1 (4.5-ounce) can chopped **green chiles**

½ cup **Simple but Epic Caramelized Onions** (page 162)

1½ cups shredded **Manchego cheese** or nondairy cheese

1 cup chunky **salsa**

Topping Ideas

Chopped avocado

Unsweetened nondairy yogurt (for "sour cream")

Lime wedges

1. Preheat the oven to 375°F and grease a 9-inch round or square baking dish with avocado oil.

2. Place a tortilla in the prepared baking dish and top it with half of the chicken, green chiles, and caramelized onions. Sprinkle ½ cup of the cheese on top, and then spoon about ¼ cup of the salsa over the cheese. Cover with another tortilla and the remaining chicken, green chiles, onions, and another ½ cup of the cheese and 1 to 2 tablespoons of the salsa. Top with the last tortilla, and sprinkle with the remaining cheese and salsa.

3. Bake until the cheese is melted, 15 to 20 minutes.

4. Remove the enchilada pie from the oven and add your desired toppings. Cut it into 4 slices and serve warm. Leftovers will keep in an airtight container in the fridge for 5 days. To reheat, cover the dish with foil and warm it in a 350°F oven for a few minutes.

To make the pie vegan, omit the chicken and use nondairy cheese.

solo meals

Be Your Own Best Friend: Quick Lunch + Dinner Combos When Cooking for One

How often do you compare yourself to others? What the girl next to you at work is having for lunch? Or the outfit your best friend is wearing versus what you have on? Or how about living a life of FOMO, watching everyone's Instagram stories, thinking their lives are so much cooler than yours? Ya, been there, done that.

It is time to get out of the comparison trap, friends. The most important relationship we will have in life is the one with ourselves, but it is also the most challenging. It took me years to figure out what being "myself" actually meant. I was always comparing my body to other girls and thinking everyone's life was more put together and "better" than mine. On social media, we see the luxurious vacations that people are on or the perfectly styled breakfast bowl. I'm guilty of portraying this, too, but I'm here to say that my life is far from perfect. Behind every recipe on my blog and book was one (or five) that failed. Preceding every success was a handful of struggles. I am not someone who runs marathons or lifts heavy weights at the gym. Nor do I enjoy drinking green juice and eating veggies all day. When I realized that perfection doesn't exist for anyone in this world and

accepted who I am, it was as if a major shift had happened in my life. I cleared out any negative energy. I stopped committing to things that I had zero desire to do. I started appreciating myself more than I ever had before. I don't compare myself to others anymore and, boy, does it feel good!

I have become my own best friend. I'm not afraid to go out to eat on my own. I love going to get a manicure by myself. I feel happy signing up for a barre class solo. These activities have helped me grow and learn who I am. I've learned to be more confident, truly love myself, and give myself the respect I deserve.

As someone who has been the outcast when it comes to food for quite some time, I have mastered healthy, easy meals for one person. In this chapter, I am sharing my absolute favorite go-to recipes for making lunch or dinner for yourself. They're going to seem so simple that you will ask yourself why you haven't been eating these meals for years. They're perfect for after work or school, when you want something easy, quick, and delicious but just need to feed one person (a.k.a. you). Don't forget to go into this chapter with your food prep complete, as it will make your solo eating life even simpler.

> it is time to fall in love with yourself and out of the comparison trap

crispy tortilla pizza
with fried eggs

Eggs are a staple in my daily diet. Whether for lunch or dinner, I toss an egg or two or three on it. This tortilla pizza with fried eggs brings together two of my favorite meals—tacos and pizza! It's perfect for whenever you need something super quick, filling, and with little to no mess involved. You can easily sub the veggies and ingredients you have on hand, too.

SERVES 1

2 teaspoons **avocado oil**

2 medium **gluten-free tortillas**

½ **avocado**

¼ cup chunky **salsa**

2 tablespoons **Simple but Epic Caramelized Onions** (page 162)

2 tablespoons **creamy goat cheese**

2 large pasture-raised **eggs**

Sea salt and **freshly ground black pepper**

¾ cup **leafy greens**, for garnish

Want more protein? Organic chicken sausage, crispy bacon, or smoked salmon would be delicious here!

1. Heat 1 teaspoon of the avocado oil in a large skillet over medium-high heat, and add the tortillas (one at a time, if necessary). Cook the tortillas on one side only for about 3 minutes. Transfer the tortillas to a cutting board (set the skillet aside for now) and stack them with the cooked sides facing each other.

2. Mash the avocado on top of the stacked tortillas, spreading it so it is evenly distributed. Spoon the salsa on top and spread it evenly. Spread the caramelized onions and goat cheese over the salsa.

3. In a small skillet, heat the remaining 1 teaspoon avocado oil over medium-high heat. Gently crack the eggs into the skillet, reduce the heat to low, and cover the skillet. Cook the eggs until done to your liking, 3 to 5 minutes.

4. While the eggs cook, return the loaded tortilla stack to the large skillet and crisp it for about 5 minutes over medium heat.

5. Once the eggs are cooked, season them with salt and pepper. Transfer the tortilla stack to a plate and slide the eggs on top. Sprinkle the greens over the eggs. Serve warm.

soba noodle veggie stir-fry

If you are still ordering lo mein from the Chinese restaurant around the corner, this recipe is for you. Save your restaurant delivery money with this simple single-serving soba stir-fry filled with veggies and a creamy nut butter sauce—a win in my book (and wallet). Craving protein? Toss in some poached chicken (page 132) or wild salmon to make it a bit more filling. Double the recipe if you want extras to take for lunch the next day.

SERVES 1

2 ounces uncooked **soba noodles**

1 tablespoon **toasted sesame oil**

½ teaspoon **minced garlic**

½ teaspoon **ground ginger**

¼ cup chopped **onion**

¼ cup chopped **bell pepper**

¼ cup **broccoli florets**

1 pasture-raised **egg**

1 tablespoon **coconut aminos**

1 tablespoon **Sriracha sauce**

1 tablespoon **creamy nut butter**

1. Fill a medium pot halfway with water and bring it to a boil. Add the soba noodles and cook until tender, about 6 minutes.

2. While the noodles cook, heat the sesame oil in a large skillet over medium heat. Add the garlic, ginger, onion, bell pepper, and broccoli. Cover the skillet and cook, stirring occasionally, until softened, about 6 minutes.

3. Strain the soba noodles and add them to the vegetables in the skillet.

4. Crack the egg into the skillet and mix well, breaking up the yolk and white and cooking it into the vegetables and noodles.

5. Once the egg starts to set, add the coconut aminos, Sriracha, and nut butter and mix well. Serve warm.

Not in the mood for soba noodles? Swap in your favorite pasta or spiralized veggie instead. Zucchini noodles are great here!

the epic
5-minute quesadilla

I don't like to pick favorites, but this super-quick quesadilla is seriously my go-to every single week. If you've prepped some veggies and protein (see page 35), it's ready in just minutes. The almond milk cream cheese is key: it adds a lot of flavor and melts much better than other nut cheeses, helping to bind the quesadilla. Fill the quesadilla with wild salmon, chicken, or ground lamb, or even throw in a crumbled veggie burger if you aren't in the mood for meat.

SERVES 1

2 medium-size **grain-free tortillas**

3 tablespoons **almond milk cream cheese** or **Herbed Cashew Cheese** (page 187)

5 to 6 ounces cooked **protein of choice** (such as Bone Broth–Poached Chicken, page 132), shredded or chopped into small pieces

¼ cup **Simple but Epic Caramelized Onions** (page 162)

½ cup fresh **baby arugula**

½ small **avocado**, chopped

1 teaspoon **avocado oil**

1. Lay the tortillas on a cutting board and gently spread the almond milk cream cheese over each one.

2. Add your preferred protein and the caramelized onions, arugula, and avocado to one tortilla. Top with the other tortilla, cream cheese–side down, and press on it so it adheres.

3. Heat the avocado oil in a large skillet over medium heat. Carefully transfer the quesadilla to the hot skillet and cook for about 5 minutes. Flip and cook until it is crispy on the other side, about 5 minutes more. Serve warm.

Got another minute? Serve the quesadilla alongside roasted veggies from your food prep.

If you're not paleo or dairy-free, creamy goat cheese is a delicious option.

creamy alfredo
zucchini noodles

If you're not already on the veggie-noodle train, you're about to go crazy, my friends. Here's the lowdown: you can pretty much spiralize any vegetable you see in the store and turn it into a spaghetti-type noodle. Butternut squash, sweet potatoes, carrots, beets, and, the most popular, zucchini are just a few of the vegetables you can spiralize or even purchase in noodle form. Zucchini is by far my favorite veggie noodle, and I love using it as a base in dishes. It's also great to combine with gluten-free noodles, or any pasta you'd like, to make it half veg and half actual noodles. And the cream sauce in this noodle bowl? It's not what you expect. I use almond milk cream cheese because it melts so perfectly into the warm noodles.

SERVES 1

1 large **zucchini**, or 2 cups prepared spiralized **zucchini noodles**

⅓ cup sliced **mushrooms**

½ tablespoon **avocado oil**

Sea salt and **freshly ground black pepper**

¼ cup **Simple but Epic Caramelized Onions** (page 162)

5 to 6 ounces cooked **protein of choice** (such as chicken or sausage crumbles)

2 tablespoons **almond milk cream cheese** or **Herbed Cashew Cheese** (page 187)

1 cup fresh **baby arugula**

2 tablespoons **pine nuts**

1. Trim both ends of the zucchini. Use a spiralizer to cut it into zucchini noodles. (Or use your store-bought spiralized zoodles.)

2. Add the zucchini noodles and mushrooms to a large skillet and drizzle the avocado oil on top. Season with salt and pepper. Cook over medium heat until the noodles are just tender, about 5 minutes (don't overcook or they will get soggy).

3. Add the caramelized onions and your cooked protein, stir to combine, and cook until heated through, 1 to 2 minutes more.

4. Transfer the mixture to a bowl and add the almond milk cream cheese, stirring until it is melted. Sprinkle the arugula and pine nuts on top. Serve warm.

waffled veggie burger

breakfast sammie

Most would think that a waffle iron is an extra, just-for-fun kind of appliance, but not in our house. If you have the room, I cannot recommend it enough. I use mine weekly to make Chocolate Chip Sweet Potato Waffles (page 69) and to "waffle" toast for breakfast sandwiches like this one. It takes your breakfast sandwich from zero to a hundred real quick. Whoever thinks breakfast can't be for dinner clearly doesn't know how delicious this waffled sammie is! It's a staple for me, especially when dining solo or making a quick lunch at home.

gf df nf

SERVES 1

½ tablespoon **avocado oil**, plus more for greasing the waffle iron

1 store-bought **veggie burger**

1 large pasture-raised **egg**

2 slices **gluten-free bread** or other bread of choice

1 to 2 tablespoons **Dijon mustard**

¾ cup **leafy greens**

2 tablespoons **nondairy cheese of choice**

½ **avocado**, sliced

1. Preheat the waffle iron according to the manufacturer's instructions and grease it with avocado oil.

2. Add the ½ tablespoon avocado oil to a small skillet and warm it over medium heat. Add the veggie burger to the hot skillet and cook until warmed through, about 4 minutes on each side.

3. Remove the veggie burger from the skillet and crack the egg into the skillet. Cover and cook until the egg is done to your liking, 4 to 5 minutes.

4. While the egg cooks, add each piece of bread to the waffle iron, press down, and cook until toasted, 1 to 2 minutes.

5. Remove the waffled bread from the waffle iron and spread both slices with the mustard. Add the cooked veggie burger, leafy greens, cheese, avocado, and egg to one waffle and top it with the other one, mustard-side down.

6. Slice the sammie in half and serve warm.

Don't have a waffle iron? Not a problem! Panini this instead by putting the prepared sandwich toppings between the slices of bread and crisping the sandwich in some hot, grass-fed butter or avocado oil in a large skillet for 3 minutes. Flip and cook for another couple of minutes, until it is browned to your liking.

every night **breakfast tacos**

Are you sensing a theme here? Ya, same. Eggs are a go-to over at our house, any time of the day. They easily add fat and protein to your meal and are a super-affordable protein option, too. Even when you buy organic pasture-raised eggs, you are getting a dozen eggs for a very reasonable amount of money. Compared to meat or fish, that is a solid deal. For these tacos, the egg style is up to you—scrambled, fried, poached, you name it. I go for poaching so the yolk bursts and gets all up in the taco, but it's totally your choice.

SERVES 1

2 medium **grain-free tortillas**

2 large **pasture-raised eggs**

2 ounces **smoked wild salmon**

1 cup **leafy greens**

½ **avocado**, sliced

3 tablespoons **almond milk cream cheese** or **Herbed Cashew Cheese** (page 187)

Everything Bagel seasoning blend (see page 46)

1. Fill a small saucepan three-quarters full with water and bring to a boil.

2. Carefully hang the tortillas over one or two rungs of an oven rack (depending on the distance between the rungs), place the rack in the oven, and set it to 350°F. The tortillas should form taco "shells" after 3 to 5 minutes.

3. While the tortillas are baking, break each egg into its own small ramekin. Gently slide the egg out of the ramekins and add to the boiling water. Reduce the heat to low so the water stays at a simmer, and poach the eggs until done to your liking, about 5 minutes for medium yolks. Gently remove the eggs with a slotted spoon and set aside on a paper towel–lined plate.

4. While the eggs poach, add the wild salmon, leafy greens, avocado, and almond milk cream cheese to the taco shells.

5. Add an egg to each filled taco shell, sprinkle with the seasoning, and enjoy warm.

queen b **beet sauce noodles**

This will be one of the most gorgeous bowls of pasta you've ever eaten. Beets make a delicious, light pesto-like sauce. Double the recipe if you want to make extra for lunch the next day, but be sure to make it in daylight so you can photograph the dreamy color!

SERVES 1

4 to 5 ounces uncooked **gluten-free pasta**

2 tablespoons **raw walnuts,** chopped

2 small cooked **beets**

1 small **garlic clove**

1 tablespoon **avocado oil**

2 tablespoons **unsweetened nondairy milk**

¼ teaspoon **sea salt**

1. Bring a medium pot of water to a boil. Add the pasta and cook according to the package instructions.

2. While the pasta cooks, toast the walnuts in a small dry skillet over medium heat until they are golden brown and fragrant, about 2 minutes.

3. Add the toasted walnuts, beets, garlic, avocado oil, nondairy milk, and salt to a food processor and blend until creamy.

4. Drain the pasta, transfer it to a bowl, top it with the beet sauce, and toss to coat. Enjoy warm or at room temperature.

Want to add some protein to this? The Mini Lamb Meatballs on page 133 are so good with this sauce.

sweet potato pizzas
with pesto sauce

Let's put this recipe on repeat, please—we'll just pretend it's a veggie-based pizza bagel! Sweet potatoes are a staple in the kitchen for a reason: you can do so much with them. This version uses pesto, but to go red-style with it, you can add marinara on top, or even get really crazy and use both sauces together. These pizzas also make an easy appetizer to serve at a dinner party—just cut them into smaller bite-size pieces for a fun finger food!

SERVES 1

Sweet Potato Pizzas

1 medium **sweet potato**, scrubbed

½ tablespoon **avocado oil**

3 tablespoons **grated cheese or nondairy cheese of choice**

Pesto Sauce

¾ cup **fresh basil leaves**

⅓ cup fresh **baby arugula**

2 to 3 tablespoons **avocado oil**

1 **garlic clove**

2 tablespoons **fresh lemon juice**

2 tablespoons **pine nuts**

Sea salt and **freshly ground black pepper**

1. Preheat the oven to 425°F and line a baking sheet with parchment paper.

2. **Cook the sweet potato:** Slice the sweet potato lengthwise into ¼-inch-thick planks.

3. Place the sweet potato pieces on the prepared baking sheet and toss with the avocado oil. Spread them out so the pieces are not touching and bake for 10 minutes.

4. **While the sweet potato pieces bake, make the pesto:** In a food processor, combine the basil, arugula, avocado oil, garlic, lemon juice, pine nuts, and salt and pepper, and blend until creamy.

5. Flip the sweet potato pieces and spread the pesto on top. Sprinkle with the cheese, return the sweet potatoes to the oven, and bake until the cheese is melted, about 5 minutes more. Serve warm. Store leftover pesto in the fridge for up to 1 week or in the freezer for up to 1 month. Make a pizza with the pesto or add the pesto to an omelet. (Don't knock it 'til you've tried it!)

Craving more protein?
I love adding some crumbled cooked sausage on top along with the cheese in step 5. Or use any cooked protein you have on hand!

veggie-loaded sheet-pan **fajitas**

Restaurant-style DIY fajitas—except better. Whenever I ate at a Chili's restaurant as a kid, I'd beg someone in the family to get the fajitas because they'd serve them on a hot skillet that came out sizzling and smelling so good. I never ordered the fajitas because I wasn't eating vegetables back then—I only wanted the sizzling meat. I'm making up for lost time with this recipe. I love that you're only going to clean one pan after making this plant-based meal (and with the parchment, you barely need to clean it at all!). You even warm the tortillas on the pan that held the veg—it is that easy!

SERVES 1

¼ cup sliced **onion**

½ cup sliced **bell pepper**

1 large **portobello mushroom**, sliced

½ teaspoon **chipotle powder**

½ teaspoon **garlic powder**

½ teaspoon **freshly ground black pepper**

½ teaspoon **sea salt**

1 tablespoon **avocado oil**

2 medium **grain-free tortillas**

½ **avocado**, diced

¼ cup chunky **salsa**

1. Preheat the oven to 400°F and line a baking sheet with parchment paper.

2. In a large bowl, combine the onion, bell pepper, mushroom, chipotle powder, garlic powder, black pepper, and salt, and mix well to coat the vegetables with the spices.

3. Drizzle the avocado oil over the vegetables and toss again to coat evenly.

4. Transfer the seasoned vegetables to the prepared baking sheet and bake until they are cooked through and starting to brown on the edges, about 30 minutes.

5. Remove the baking sheet from the oven and transfer the vegetables to a medium bowl. Place the tortillas on the baking sheet and warm them in the oven, 3 to 5 minutes.

6. Fill the tortillas with the vegetables, avocado, and salsa, and serve warm.

Want some extra protein?
Throw in some poached chicken (see page 132) or cooked ground grass-fed beef to make this meal even more filling.

creamy sweet potato
mac + cheese in a mug

Want something cozy and quick that you can eat on the couch while watching *Real Housewives*? And that doesn't dirty the entire kitchen? Same! This creamy mac and cheese is made in a mug . . . in your microwave! It is crazy easy and delicious. I am over the whole "microwaves are bad for you" deal. They are a convenient option for reheating food and quickly cooking things like this pasta. You will be licking the fork clean when you finish this dish. (I wish I had thought of this back when I was eating Kraft Easy Mac in college!) For a fuller meal, treat it as a side dish or top it with some protein.

v **gf** **df** **nf**

SERVES 1

½ cup uncooked **gluten-free short pasta** (penne and elbows work best)

3 tablespoons **unsweetened nondairy milk**

1 teaspoon **gluten-free tapioca flour**

3 tablespoons **sweet potato puree** (see page 238)

¼ teaspoon **garlic powder**

¼ teaspoon **freshly ground black pepper**

¼ teaspoon **sea salt**

1 tablespoon **nutritional yeast**

1. In a large microwave-safe mug or soup bowl, combine the pasta and ¾ cup water.

2. Microwave the mixture, stirring it every minute to keep the water from overflowing, until the pasta is tender, 3 to 5 minutes.

3. Drain the pasta and return it to the mug. Add the nondairy milk, tapioca flour, sweet potato puree, garlic powder, pepper, salt, and nutritional yeast and stir to combine.

4. Microwave for another 30 seconds to let the sauce thicken. Stir well. If the sauce is still too thin, microwave for 15 to 30 seconds more. Serve warm.

For a bit of protein, toss in some cooked ground meat or Bone Broth Poached Chicken (page 132) after the mac and cheese is cooked.

let's toast

I love that something as basic as toast is so versatile. You can use any bread you'd like, from sourdough to sprouted, to gluten-free to paleo. We head to a local bakery or farmers' market on weekends and stock up, or we find a high-quality loaf in the grocery store. I used to be intimidated when buying a large loaf of bread because it would turn stale quickly, but now we freeze what's left after a couple of days and toast it up as we eat.

Here are my favorite quick combos to enjoy at any time of day.

That's My Jam

Nut butter, sliced caramelized banana, blueberry chia jam (see page 93) + sprinkled granola

Better Than a Pizza Bagel

Tomato sauce, sliced cooked chicken sausage, nondairy or dairy cheese, roasted mushrooms (see page 169) + basil (broil this baby *up*!)

Hello, Halloumi

Pesto (see page 217), grilled halloumi cheese, 2 soft-boiled eggs, toasted pine nuts + baby spinach

Veggies on Veggies →

Almond milk cream cheese,
sliced avocado, roasted mushrooms
(see page 169), veggie burger +
leafy greens

Gone Greek

Hummus, mashed avocado,
feta or nut cheese, baby
arugula, sliced olives + eggs
(fried, scrambled, poached,
or hard-boiled)

desserts

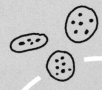

Finding the Happy Place in Your Body: Have Your Gluten-Free Cake and Eat It Too

Do you know many women who don't complain about *some* part of their appearance? Ya, same. We put so much pressure on ourselves to look a certain way and fit into a particular size jean. We compare our bodies to those around us instead of being grateful for the one we have. It is not a healthy way to live.

Everyone feels stressed or overwhelmed by food at times. I surely do. I have been twenty-five-plus pounds more than I am today and twenty-five pounds less (not including pregnancy!). Both ends of the spectrum come with their challenges. A size doesn't define us. Being very thin and skinny was a dream of mine, until I got there and then I was miserable. No clothes fit me well and I had to shop in the girls' section in stores. I was afraid of a piece of bread. I have been on crazy grain-free and sugar-free diets in which I couldn't even eat a banana, and I was the crankiest person on the planet. I have counted calories, macros, and all of that brainwashing math.

It took me more than twenty-eight years to look in a mirror and love what I see. Now, that doesn't mean that I think what I see is perfect. But instead of being self-critical, I have found my happy place in my body. I look in the mirror with confidence and am grateful to have the body I was given. I have accepted myself in any shape or form, especially post-pregnancy. My body is a warrior. It has been through hell and back between my weight fluctuations, infertility treatments, and pregnancy, and I'm grateful to my body for handling it all.

I am proud to say that I no longer restrict foods that I want to eat. I never miss out on eating dessert every day. There is a reason why my recipes don't come with a nutritional breakdown: I don't want those numbers to be the center of it all. I want to eat food and see how I feel and how it fuels me, then allow that to inform whether or not I eat it again.

You won't find me going on a juice cleanse or starting a diet. I am thankful those days are over. Instead, I focus on eating whole foods that fuel and energize me—as food is supposed to.

Since I prioritize eating dessert every day (yes, every day), I have plenty of sweet treats in my arsenal. There are many cookies to choose from. There is nothing more satisfying and comforting to me than closing out the day with a glass of almond milk and a couple of warm cookies, and not worrying about whether or not my jeans will fit me tomorrow. Have the cookie, enjoy it, and go stand in front of the mirror and tell yourself you are flipping gorgeous. Chocolate on your face and all.

> Have the cookie, enjoy it, and go tell yourself you are flipping gorgeous

extra-fudgy
zucchini bread blondies

Anything zucchini is the way to my heart. I love zucchini muffins, zucchini loaves, and especially these fudgy squares that combine two of our favorite desserts into one recipe: zucchini bread meets blondies. They are soft, flavorful, and lightly sweetened with coconut sugar. If you added some coconut yogurt and granola on top, the blondies would make a delicious breakfast!

MAKES 9 BLONDIES

¼ cup **liquid coconut oil**, plus more for greasing the baking dish

½ cup **unsweetened applesauce**

3 tablespoons **pure maple syrup**

1 teaspoon **pure vanilla extract**

⅓ cup **unsweetened nondairy milk**

1 cup shredded **zucchini**

1¾ cups **gluten-free oat flour**

⅓ cup **coconut sugar**

1 teaspoon **ground cinnamon**

1 teaspoon **baking powder**

⅓ cup **dairy-free dark chocolate chips**

⅓ cup coarsely chopped **raw walnuts**

1. Preheat the oven to 375°F and grease an 8-inch square baking dish with coconut oil.

2. In a large bowl, combine the coconut oil, applesauce, maple syrup, vanilla, and nondairy milk.

3. Wrap the zucchini in paper towels or a kitchen towel and squeeze out any excess moisture. Add the zucchini to the wet ingredients in the bowl. Add the oat flour, coconut sugar, cinnamon, and baking powder and mix well. Fold in the dark chocolate chips and walnuts and pour the batter into the prepared baking dish.

4. Bake until the edges are golden and the blondies are cooked through when tested with a toothpick, 40 to 45 minutes. Let the blondies cool for a few minutes in the baking dish before slicing into 9 squares. Store leftover blondies in an airtight container at room temperature for up to 5 days, or in the freezer for up to 2 months.

pillowy almond flour
sugar cookies

These are hands down the best cookie for any baking session: holidays, middle of summer, whenever the craving strikes. These are the ultimate coconut sugar-sweetened cookie, made with almond and coconut flours for extra protein and healthy fat. I actually prefer these cookies now over traditional sugar cookies—they are so satisfying and easy to make! I know it is annoying to have to refrigerate dough, but I do recommend doing so for this recipe—you won't regret having used a little extra patience when you bite into these heavenly, pillowy cookies.

MAKES 18 TO 20 COOKIES

½ cup (1 stick) grass-fed **butter**, at room temperature

¾ cup **coconut sugar**

2 large pasture-raised **eggs**, at room temperature

2 teaspoons **pure vanilla extract**

1 teaspoon **baking powder**

2½ cups blanched **almond flour**

½ cup **coconut flour**

Don't want to use almond flour? Sub 2¼ cups oat flour or spelt flour.

1. In a large bowl, cream the butter and coconut sugar together with an electric hand mixer until fluffy. Add the eggs and vanilla and mix until well combined.

2. In a medium bowl, mix together the baking powder, almond flour, and coconut flour until combined.

3. Add half of the dry ingredients to the wet ingredients and beat with the mixer until combined. Add the rest of the dry ingredients and beat again until incorporated.

4. Form the dough into a ball in the bowl, cover the bowl with a kitchen towel, and chill it in the refrigerator for about 30 minutes.

5. Preheat the oven to 350°F and line a baking sheet with parchment paper (if you have two sheets, line them both).

6. Scooping about 2 tablespoons of the dough at a time, roll the dough into balls and then flatten them a bit, to about 1 inch (not too much so the cookies stay pillowy when baking). Place the cookies on the prepared baking sheet(s), leaving about 1 inch between them.

7. Bake until light golden brown, 13 to 15 minutes. Let the cookies cool for about 10 minutes before removing them from the baking sheet. These cookies will keep in an airtight container at room temperature for up to 5 days, or in the freezer for up to 5 months.

crunchy **chocolate chip cookie sticks**

Even though I'm a girl who usually prefers a thick, softer cookie, I am truly obsessed with these cookie sticks. They have the most perfect crunch factor and are the best for dipping into your coffee or nut milk. Plus, my amazing tribe helped me find a name for them when I posted a teaser on Instagram, and when I saw how excited you were for these cookies, I couldn't *not* include them in the book! Once you take your first bite, you will see why there is so much excitement around these gems.

MAKES ABOUT 24 COOKIE STICKS

1 cup **coconut sugar**

½ cup **liquid coconut oil**

½ cup **creamy nut butter**

1 large pasture-raised **egg**

1 teaspoon **pure vanilla extract**

1 cup blanched **almond flour**

⅓ cup **gluten-free tapioca flour**

2 teaspoons **DIY Paleo Baking Powder** (page 29)

¾ cup **dairy-free dark chocolate chips**

1 teaspoon **sea salt**

> **Don't have almond flour?** Sub in 1 cup oat flour or spelt flour.
>
> **Don't have coconut oil?** Use melted grass-fed butter or ghee (see page 30).

1. Preheat the oven to 350°F and line a baking sheet with parchment paper.

2. In a large bowl, cream together the coconut sugar, coconut oil, nut butter, egg, and vanilla with an electric hand mixer until well combined.

3. In a small bowl, combine the almond flour, tapioca flour, and baking powder and mix well.

4. Add the dry ingredients to the wet ingredients and mix with a hand mixer or a spatula until well combined. Fold in the dark chocolate chips.

5. Scoop the dough onto the prepared baking sheet and use your hands or a spatula to form it into a large, narrow rectangle about 8 × 11 inches or so and ½ inch thick. Sprinkle the salt on top.

6. Bake until the edges are golden brown, 15 to 18 minutes. Allow the cookie to cool on the baking sheet for about 15 minutes, and then cut it into smaller rectangles, about 3 × 1 inches. These cookies will keep in an airtight container at room temperature for 5 days, or in the freezer for up to 2 months.

Don't feel like
using oat flour?
Sub in 1 cup
sprouted spelt
flour instead.

extra-chocolatey
chocolate lava cakes

Whenever I eat these chocolate lava cakes, I think of my no-so-little-anymore brother, Seth. He is the biggest fan of this dessert ever and was definitely impressed with my homemade lava cakes. Don't be intimidated by the idea of making your own—I did a happy dance around my kitchen once I saw how simple this is.

v · **gf** · **df** · **nf**

MAKES 8 CAKES

3 tablespoons **liquid coconut oil**, plus more for greasing the pan

⅓ cup **cacao powder**, plus more for dusting the pan

¾ cup **unsweetened nondairy milk**, at room temperature

1 teaspoon **apple cider vinegar**

1 cup **dairy-free dark chocolate chips**

¾ teaspoon **pure vanilla extract**

½ cup **coconut sugar**

¾ cup **unsweetened applesauce**

1 cup **gluten-free oat flour**

¾ teaspoon **baking powder**

8 (1-ounce) squares **dairy-free dark chocolate** (Hu's Salty Dark Chocolate is my fave)

1. Preheat the oven to 350°F. Grease 8 cups of a 12-cup muffin pan with a bit of coconut oil and then dust them with cacao powder.

2. In a large bowl, combine the nondairy milk and apple cider vinegar. Let the mixture sit for about 5 minutes.

3. In a small saucepan, melt the chocolate chips over medium-low heat. Stir until completely melted. Remove from the heat.

4. Add the coconut oil, vanilla, coconut sugar, and applesauce to the milk and vinegar, and mix well with a whisk or electric hand mixer. Add the cacao powder, oat flour, and baking powder and mix again until there are no lumps. Stir in about half of the melted chocolate.

5. Fill each prepared muffin cup with ¼ cup of the batter and place a square of chocolate in the middle of each cup, gently pushing it down into the batter. Top with the rest of the batter, making sure the chocolate squares are covered.

6. Bake until a toothpick inserted in the side of a cake comes out clean (inserting it in the center will not work since the toothpick will prick the melted chocolate square), 15 to 17 minutes. Let the cakes sit for about 5 minutes. Invert a large baking sheet over the muffin pan, carefully flip the pan, and lift it off to release. Top with the remaining melted chocolate and serve immediately. Leftover lava cakes will keep in the fridge for 5 days. Reheat them in the microwave in 15-second increments.

3-ingredient thumbprint cookies
with homemade berry chia jam

This is one of the easiest recipes in the book. The cookies call for only three ingredients and are topped off with a homemade berry chia jam—they are too good. Making your own jam sounds one hundred times harder than it actually is, by the way. I love making jam from scratch because I know the fruit is organic and the jam will be low in sugar—plus, it saves money. To make easy even easier, you can make this jam the night before you bake the cookies! You can keep any leftover jam for a PB&J or smear it on toast the next day.

MAKES ABOUT 16 COOKIES

Cookies

1¼ cups blanched **almond flour**

¼ cup **liquid coconut oil**

3 tablespoons **pure maple syrup**

Berry Chia Jam

½ cup fresh **berries** (blueberries or raspberries work best!)

1 tablespoon **pure maple syrup**

2 tablespoons **fresh lemon juice**

1 tablespoon **chia seeds**

1. **Make the cookie dough:** In a large bowl, mix together the almond flour, coconut oil, and maple syrup. Cover the bowl with a kitchen towel and chill it in the fridge for about 30 minutes.

2. **Meanwhile, make the jam:** Add the berries and maple syrup to a small saucepan set over medium heat. Mash the berries with a fork and stir until they form a sauce. Add the lemon juice and chia seeds and cook until the jam thickens, about 5 minutes. Remove the pan from the heat and let the jam cool for at least 10 minutes.

3. Preheat the oven to 350°F and line a baking sheet with parchment paper.

4. Roll the chilled dough into 15 to 16 balls and place them on the prepared baking sheet.

5. Press down in the center of each cookie with your thumb or a spoon to form an indentation. Fill each indentation with the jam.

6. Bake the cookies until they start to brown on the bottoms, about 10 minutes. Allow the cookies to cool on the baking sheet for a few minutes before serving. Store these cookies in an airtight container at room temperature for up to 5 days, or in the freezer for up to 2 months.

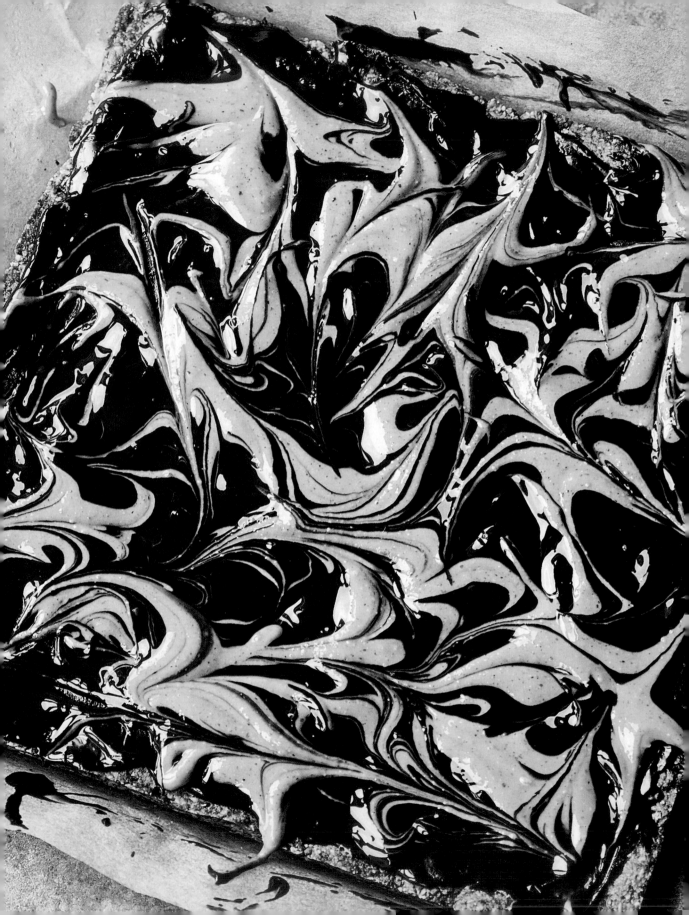

sea salt dark chocolate
peanut butter bars

There are few things in this world that I love more than the combo of chocolate and peanut butter. (Okay, fine, sweet potatoes are a close call.) These bars are rich and flavorful and have a delicious graham cracker-like cookie crust made with almond flour. The look of this dessert always mesmerizes me. Like literally—that dark chocolate and peanut butter swirl is hypnotizing. After one bite, you will go absolutely craz-ay.

MAKES 9 BARS

2 cups blanched **almond flour**

1 tablespoon **coconut flour**

⅓ cup **coconut sugar**

2 teaspoons **ground cinnamon**

2 teaspoons **DIY Paleo Baking Powder** (page 29)

3 tablespoons **liquid coconut oil**

1 large pasture-raised **egg**

1 teaspoon **pure vanilla extract**

½ cup **dairy-free dark chocolate chips**, melted (I like Hu Baking Gems in these!)

6 tablespoons **creamy peanut butter**

1 teaspoon **sea salt**

1. Preheat the oven to 300°F and line an 8-inch square baking dish with parchment paper.

2. In a large bowl, mix together the almond flour, coconut flour, coconut sugar, cinnamon, and baking powder. Add the coconut oil, egg, and vanilla and mix well until the dough comes together.

3. Transfer the dough to the prepared baking dish and press down on it to form a level crust.

4. Bake until the crust begins to turn golden, about 15 minutes. Remove the baking dish from the oven (leave the oven on) and spread the melted chocolate evenly over the crust. Dollop the peanut butter on top of the chocolate. Using a toothpick or a very sharp knife, swirl the peanut butter and chocolate to create a marbled effect. Sprinkle the salt over the top.

5. Return the baking dish to the oven and bake until the bars are cooked through, about 15 minutes. Let the bars cool in the dish for at least 20 minutes to let the crust set before slicing it into 9 pieces. Any extra bars will keep in an airtight container at room temperature for up to 5 days, or in the freezer for up to 2 months.

sweet potato
almond butter brownies

Just go with me on this one, you guys! Sweet potatoes in brownies? So awkward, but so underrated. You'd never know there is sweet potato in here, I swear. They add the best texture to the brownies, making them extra moist and fudgy. I highly recommend eating these while they are warm because there is nothing better than a hot, gooey brownie with melted chocolate chips in the center! Add a scoop of your favorite ice cream on top for an at-home brownie à la mode.

MAKES 9 BROWNIES

¼ cup **liquid coconut oil**, plus more for greasing the baking dish

1 cup **sweet potato puree** (see Note)

½ cup **creamy almond butter**

1 teaspoon **pure vanilla extract**

½ cup **unsweetened nondairy milk**

1½ cups **gluten-free oat flour**

⅓ cup **cacao powder**

¼ cup **coconut sugar**

½ teaspoon **baking powder**

½ cup **dairy-free dark chocolate chips**

1. Preheat the oven to 375°F and grease an 8-inch square baking dish with coconut oil.

2. In a large bowl, combine the sweet potato puree, almond butter, coconut oil, vanilla, and nondairy milk. Add the oat flour, cacao powder, coconut sugar, and baking powder, and mix well to combine. Fold in the dark chocolate chips.

3. Transfer the batter to the prepared baking dish and bake until a toothpick inserted in the center comes out clean, 30 to 35 minutes. Let the brownies cool in the dish for 10 to 15 minutes. Slice into 9 pieces and serve. Store any leftover brownies in an airtight container in the fridge for up to 5 days, or in the freezer for up to 2 months. I usually warm them up in the microwave before eating.

To make the sweet potato puree, remove the skin from one roasted sweet potato. Place the sweet potato in a food processor and pulse until smooth. You can also buy ready-made sweet potato puree.

mini chocolate chip cookie cups
with chocolate ganache centers

Have you ever eaten a chocolate chip cookie and wished there was more chocolate in there? Yes, same. Here's the dream solution: mini cookie cups filled with a rich dark chocolate ganache made from dark chocolate chips and coconut milk. They pretty much take your average cookie up a hundred notches.

MAKES 24 CUPS

1½ cups **gluten-free oat flour**

1 teaspoon **baking powder**

½ cup **liquid coconut oil**

⅓ cup **coconut sugar**

1 **flax egg** (page 29)

3 teaspoons **pure vanilla extract**

1 cup **dairy-free dark chocolate chips**

7 ounces (½ can) **full-fat coconut milk**

⅓ cup **cacao powder**

1. Preheat the oven to 350°F and line a 24-cup mini muffin pan with paper liners.

2. In a medium bowl, combine the oat flour and baking powder.

3. In a large bowl, combine the coconut oil, coconut sugar, flax egg, and vanilla, and beat with an electric hand mixer until well combined and creamy. Add the flour mixture to the wet ingredients and mix again until the dough is well combined. Fold in ½ cup of the dark chocolate chips.

4. Scoop about a tablespoon of the dough into each lined muffin cup and press it down. Bake until just golden, about 10 minutes. Remove from the oven and leave the oven on.

5. Using a teaspoon-size measuring spoon, press down in the center of each cookie to form an indentation.

6. In a small saucepan, whisk together the coconut milk and cacao powder over low heat until smooth. Spoon some of the ganache into the indentation in each cookie. (Save any leftover ganache to drizzle at the end!)

7. Return the muffin pan to the oven and bake until the centers are set, 10 to 12 minutes. Let the cups cool in the pan for 15 to 20 minutes, then sprinkle the remaining chocolate chips on top. Transfer the muffin pan to the fridge for about 20 minutes to let the cookie cups set before serving. Extra cookie cups will keep in an airtight container at room temperature for up to 5 days, or in the freezer for up to 2 months.

classic gluten-free
chocolate chip cookies

Is there anything better than chocolate chip cookies? I crave them pretty much on the regular. After we finish dinner, I sprint to the counter, pantry, or freezer (wherever the goods are) and check out what I have in inventory. Ninety-nine percent of the time I have these cookies on hand. They are my take on the classic chocolate chip cookie. Their consistency is on point—a soft, gooey center (especially when fresh out of the oven) and a crunchy edge all around the cookie. Plus, they even taste amazing frozen (just sayin'). Dip one in your favorite nondairy milk—you will be in heaven!

v **gf** **df**

MAKES ABOUT 18 COOKIES

⅓ cup solid **coconut oil**, softened but not melted (Garden of Life is my fave)

¾ cup **coconut sugar**

2 teaspoons **pure vanilla extract**

2 tablespoons **unsweetened nondairy milk**

1 cup blanched **almond flour**

1 cup **gluten-free oat flour**

1½ teaspoons **baking powder**

½ cup **dairy-free dark chocolate chips**

2 teaspoons **sea salt**

1. Preheat the oven to 350°F and line a baking sheet with parchment paper.

2. In a large bowl, mix together the coconut oil and coconut sugar with an electric hand mixer or a spatula. Add the vanilla and nondairy milk and mix again until well combined. Add the almond flour, oat flour, and baking powder, and mix well. If the dough is crumbly, add a splash more of nondairy milk. Fold in the dark chocolate chips.

3. Roll 1½ to 2 tablespoons of dough at a time into balls and place them about 1 inch apart on the prepared baking sheet. Flatten each ball slightly and sprinkle the salt on top.

4. Bake until golden brown, 10 to 12 minutes. Allow the cookies to cool for a few minutes on the baking sheet before serving. These cookies will keep in an airtight container at room temperature for up to 5 days, or in the freezer for up to 2 months.

coconut sugar–dusted
snickerdoodles

Snickerdoodles are one of the most underrated cookies out there. I absolutely love them (I am a sucker for anything cinnamon!) and they're always my go-to cookie order at a bakery. My dining hall in college would serve them and, oh my gosh, I used to put "extras" in my bag and keep them in my dorm room (oops!). These gluten-free vegan snickerdoodles are almost too good to be true. They are refined sugar-free but still taste sweet and delicious—perfect to dip into a cup of nondairy milk.

MAKES ABOUT 12 COOKIES

Cookies

1 cup blanched **almond flour**

1 cup **gluten-free oat flour**

1 teaspoon **ground cinnamon**

1 teaspoon **baking powder**

⅓ cup **liquid coconut oil**

½ cup **coconut sugar**

1 tablespoon **pure vanilla extract**

3 tablespoons **unsweetened nondairy milk**

Sugar Coating

2 tablespoons **coconut sugar**

1 teaspoon **ground cinnamon**

1. Preheat the oven to 350°F and line a baking sheet with parchment paper.

2. **Make the cookies:** In a medium bowl, combine the almond flour, oat flour, cinnamon, and baking powder, and mix well.

3. In a large bowl, combine the coconut oil, coconut sugar, vanilla, and nondairy milk, and mix well. Add the dry ingredients to the wet ingredients and mix until well combined.

4. Scoop 1 to 2 tablespoons of dough at a time into your hands and roll them into balls. Place the balls on the prepared baking sheet, spacing them about 1 inch apart, and flatten each one with your palm to about 1-inch thickness.

5. **Make the sugar coating:** In a small bowl, mix together the coconut sugar and cinnamon. Sprinkle each cookie with the coating mixture.

6. Bake the cookies until the edges are golden and the center is still a bit soft, 10 to 12 minutes. Let the cookies cool on the baking sheet for about 5 minutes before serving. Leftover cookies will keep in an airtight container at room temperature for up to 5 days, or in the freezer for up to 2 months.

homemade **dark chocolate caramel candy bars**

Jord's absolute favorite candy is a Snickers bar, and now I can give him this homemade dark chocolate version. A plant-based, grain-free way to eat Snickers without getting a sugar high? Yeah, baby, that's right! (Too bad they don't sell these bars for Halloween trick-or-treating.) Enjoy the dreamy caramel layer made from dates (my go-to for caramel replacement). Pro Tip: If you want to take these up a notch, add a thin layer of nut butter after the caramel layer has set.

MAKES 16 BARS

Nougat Cookie Layer

5 tablespoons **liquid coconut oil**, plus more for greasing the pan

2 cups blanched **almond flour**

3 tablespoons **coconut flour**

2 tablespoons **pure maple syrup**

1 teaspoon **pure vanilla extract**

Caramel Layer

10 pitted **Medjool dates**

1 cup hot **filtered water**

1 cup **creamy nut butter**

3 tablespoons **liquid coconut oil**

1 cup unsalted **raw nuts**, chopped

Chocolate Layer

½ cup **liquid coconut oil**

¼ cup **pure maple syrup**

⅔ cup **cacao powder**

1. **Make the cookie layer:** Preheat the oven to 350°F, and grease an 8-inch square baking dish with coconut oil or line it with parchment paper.

2. In a large bowl, stir together the almond flour, coconut flour, coconut oil, maple syrup, and vanilla until the mixture is well combined and forms a dough.

3. Place the dough in the prepared baking dish, pressing down with a spatula to form an even layer, and bake until it is golden brown, about 20 minutes. Allow it to cool for a few minutes.

4. **While the cookie layer bakes, make the caramel layer:** Add the dates to a medium bowl and cover them with the hot water. Let the dates soften for 7 to 10 minutes, then drain.

5. Add the dates, nut butter, and coconut oil to a food processor and process until fully combined (the mixture will be a bit sticky).

6. Transfer the date mixture to a large bowl and fold in the nuts with a wooden spoon.

7. Once the cookie base has cooled, evenly spread the caramel over it. Put it in the freezer to set, about 30 minutes.

8. Slice the cookie base into 16 bars and return it to the freezer to chill for 30 minutes more.

9. **Make the chocolate layer:** Combine the coconut oil, maple syrup, and cacao powder in a small saucepan, and stir over medium heat until fully combined.

10. Line a baking sheet that will fit in your freezer with parchment paper.

11. Using two forks, dip each bar in the chocolate mixture so it is coated all over. Let the excess chocolate drip off and place the bar on the parchment-lined sheet. Once all the bars are coated, place the baking sheet in the freezer to chill until the chocolate layer is set, about 1 hour. The bars will keep in an airtight container in the freezer for up to 2 months. Allow them to thaw for about 5 minutes before eating.

toasted coconut + quinoa
chocolate bark

I eat a piece (or two . . . or three . . .) of dark chocolate every single day. This unique bark is crunchy, has no added sugar, and is filled with delicious pieces of coconut flakes throughout. My dad loves this recipe—he is a dessert-before-dinner kind of guy and would totally pop a few pieces of it before his meal at night. And after, too, of course.

SERVES 5

¹⁄₃ cup uncooked **quinoa**

2 teaspoons **liquid coconut oil**

¹⁄₃ cup **unsweetened coconut flakes**

16 ounces **unsweetened dairy-free dark chocolate** (broken into pieces if needed)

1. Choose a baking sheet that will fit in your freezer and line it with parchment paper.

2. Thoroughly rinse and drain the quinoa in a strainer.

3. Heat 1 teaspoon of the coconut oil in a medium saucepan over medium-low heat. Add the quinoa (it's okay if it's still a bit wet), and using a whisk, stir the quinoa around in the pan for about 3 minutes as it starts to toast. Once the water is absorbed and the quinoa begins to make a "pop" noise, remove the pan from the heat and continue to stir until the quinoa is golden and smells nutty, about 5 minutes more. Transfer the quinoa to a large bowl and set aside.

4. In the same pan, heat the remaining 1 teaspoon coconut oil over medium-low heat. Add the coconut flakes and toast until they are golden brown, 5 to 7 minutes. Add the coconut flakes to the bowl of quinoa.

5. In a clean medium saucepan, melt the dark chocolate over medium heat, stirring frequently. Once the chocolate is smooth and fully melted, pour it into the bowl and stir well to coat the quinoa and coconut flakes. Pour the chocolate bark mixture onto the prepared baking sheet, spreading it out evenly with a spatula.

6. Place the baking sheet in the freezer to set for about 1 hour. Once it has hardened, break the bark into pieces and enjoy. It will keep in the freezer for up to 2 months. I love munching on it straight from the freezer!

fig + honey cashew
cheesecake bars

 One of my favorite chocolate-less desserts, these cheesecake bars have the perfect amount of sweetness from the fresh figs, and they're grain- and dairy-free, too. The crust is made of almonds instead of wheat flour, and in place of cream cheese or dairy, we are using raw cashews, which turn into a creamy filling. I served these at a family dinner when testing them, and the crowd went wild—I think you will too.

p **gf** **df**

MAKES 9 BARS

Crust

Liquid **coconut oil**, for greasing the baking dish

1¼ cups pitted **Medjool dates**

1 cup boiling **filtered water**

1¼ cups **raw almonds**

2 tablespoons **flaxseed meal**

Cashew Filling

1⅓ cups **raw cashews**

1 cup hot **filtered water**

¼ cup **manuka honey** (I like Wedderspoon's)

1 tablespoon **liquid coconut oil**

1 teaspoon **pure vanilla extract**

2 tablespoons **unsweetened nondairy milk**

Topping

⅓ cup sliced **fresh figs**

1 teaspoon **sea salt**

1. **Make the crust:** Preheat the oven to 400°F and grease an 8-inch square baking dish with coconut oil.

2. In a medium heatproof bowl, soak the dates in the boiling water for about 10 minutes, then drain.

3. In a food processor, pulse the dates, almonds, and flaxseed meal until well combined and a dough forms.

4. Transfer the dough to the prepared baking dish and press down on it to form an even layer for the crust. Bake until golden, about 20 minutes.

5. While the crust is baking, make the filling: In a medium bowl, soak the cashews in the hot water for about 20 minutes, then drain.

6. Place the drained cashews in a food processor and add the honey, coconut oil, vanilla, and nondairy milk, and pulse until the filling is smooth and creamy.

7. Remove the baking dish from the oven and let the crust cool for about 15 minutes.

8. Pour the cheesecake filling over the cooled crust and spread it out evenly with a spatula. Top with the sliced figs and sprinkle with the salt.

9. Freeze the bars for at least 30 minutes, or until ready to slice and serve. Store leftover bars in an airtight container in the freezer for up to 2 months.

melt-in-your-mouth
brownie batter cupcakes

We are combining two of life's greatest treats in this recipe—brownies and cupcakes—into one rich and fudgy dessert. They basically melt in your mouth when you eat them fresh out of the oven and are the ultimate crowd-pleaser for any occasion, holiday, birthday, or that random Wednesday when you are solo and craving a chocolate-y something.

MAKES 12 CUPCAKES

1 cup **liquid coconut oil**, plus more for greasing the muffin cups

1½ cups blanched **almond flour**

½ cup **cacao powder**

⅓ cup **coconut sugar**

1 teaspoon **DIY Paleo Baking Powder** (page 29)

½ cup chopped **dairy-free dark chocolate**

1 teaspoon **pure vanilla extract**

2 **flax eggs** (see page 29)

1¼ cups **boiling water**

1 teaspoon **sea salt**

2 tablespoons **cacao nibs**

1. Preheat the oven to 350°F and grease the cups of a 12-cup muffin pan with coconut oil, or line them with paper liners.

2. In a medium bowl, mix together the almond flour, cacao powder, coconut sugar, and baking powder.

3. In a small saucepan set over medium heat, melt the coconut oil, dark chocolate, and vanilla, stirring frequently, until smooth and creamy, 1 to 2 minutes.

4. Add the flax eggs, melted chocolate mixture, and boiling water to the dry ingredients and mix well.

5. Fill each muffin cup about two-thirds full with the batter and sprinkle the tops with the salt and cacao nibs.

6. Bake until a toothpick inserted in the center of a cupcake comes out clean, 20 to 25 minutes. Cool cupcakes in the pan before serving. Leftover cupcakes will keep in an airtight container at room temperature for up to 5 days, or in the freezer for up to 2 months.

Allergic to nuts?
Sub 1⅓ cups gluten-free oat flour or spelt flour for the almond flour.

Not feeling the flax eggs? Please do not substitute pasture-raised eggs here! The boiling water that's added to the batter will cook them. Instead use chia eggs (see page 29).

layered chocolate chip cookie cake
with avocado cacao cream frosting

I will forever be requesting this chocolate chip cookie cake for dessert on my birthday. Now, I just need to convince Jord or my mom to make it for me! Cookies are by far my favorite type of dessert, as you may have noticed in this chapter, but there is nothing I love more than eating a slice (or two) of this cookie cake with its rich avocado cacao cream frosting. It tastes almost too good to be vegan and gluten- and grain-free. I've also decided that if I weren't already married, this would absolutely be my wedding cake. Vow renewals, Jord? It's perfect for any special occasion or just when the craving strikes in the middle of the week.

SERVES 6 TO 8

Chocolate Chip Cookie Cake

½ cup **liquid coconut oil**, plus more for greasing the pans

¾ cup **creamy nut butter**

¾ cup **unsweetened applesauce**

3 **flax eggs** (see page 29)

3 teaspoons **pure vanilla extract**

5 cups blanched **almond flour**

⅔ cup **coconut sugar**

3 teaspoons **DIY Paleo Baking Powder** (page 29)

⅔ cup **dairy-free dark chocolate chips**

Avocado Cacao Cream Frosting

2 medium **avocados**, peeled and pitted

¼ cup **unsweetened nondairy milk**

⅓ cup **pure maple syrup**

¼ cup **coconut sugar**

⅓ cup **cacao powder**

1. **Make the cookie cake:** Preheat the oven to 350°F and grease two 8-inch round baking dishes with coconut oil.

2. In a large bowl, use a hand mixer to cream together the nut butter, coconut oil, applesauce, flax eggs, and vanilla until combined. Add the almond flour, coconut sugar, and baking powder, and mix well. Fold in the chocolate chips. Divide the batter between the prepared baking dishes.

3. Bake until a toothpick inserted in the center of a cake comes out clean, about 40 minutes. Let the cakes cool in the baking dishes.

4. **Make the frosting:** Add the avocados, nondairy milk, maple syrup, coconut sugar, and cacao powder to a food processor, and pulse until the mixture is smooth. If the frosting is too thick, add more nondairy milk as needed.

5. Once the cakes have cooled completely, gently remove them from the baking dishes and place one layer on a cake stand right-side up. Spread an even layer of frosting over the cake. Place the other cake on top right-side up and spread it with frosting. Spread the frosting on the sides of the cake as well, if desired. Freeze leftover cake for up to 2 months, and then stand at your kitchen counter at midnight, eating it and pretending it's your leftover wedding cake.

Prepping this cake ahead of time? It tastes best within the first 2 days.

white chocolate
carrot cake truffles

Okay, let's talk about white chocolate. Who here genuinely enjoys the taste of white chocolate? I personally have never been a fan of it, but then I made these carrot cake truffles with a healthier, less sweet "white chocolate" coating—and they are so good! They're also vegan, gluten-free, paleo, and perfect to bring to work, school, or a party. If you have friends who aren't huge dark chocolate fans and prefer other sweets, these are a great option to serve to them. And kids love them, too! You don't even taste the snuck in carrots, which is a win in my dessert-eating book.

MAKES 12 TO 16 TRUFFLES

Truffle Filling

10 small pitted **Medjool dates**

1 cup hot **filtered water**

1 cup coarsely grated **carrots**

2 tablespoons **coconut flour**

1 teaspoon **pure vanilla extract**

2 tablespoons **liquid coconut oil**

White Chocolate Coating

½ cup **cacao butter**

2 tablespoons **liquid coconut oil**

¼ cup **unsweetened nondairy milk**

1 tablespoon **creamy nut butter**

¼ cup **manuka honey** (I like Wedderspoon's)

1 teaspoon **pure vanilla extract**

1. **Make the truffle filling:** Place the dates in a small bowl and cover them with the hot water. Soak for about 5 minutes, then drain.

2. Add the soaked dates, carrots, coconut flour, vanilla, and coconut oil to a food processor and pulse until well combined.

3. Using a spoon or your hands, roll about 2 tablespoons of the truffle dough at a time into balls and place them on a baking sheet lined with parchment paper. Chill the truffles in the fridge until set, about 45 minutes.

4. **While the truffles chill, make the white chocolate coating:** Add the cacao butter, coconut oil, and nondairy milk to a medium heatproof bowl.

5. Place the bowl over a small pot of simmering water (don't allow the bowl to touch the water) and heat it, stirring occasionally, until the mixture is melted. Remove the bowl from the heat. Add the nut butter, honey, and vanilla and mix to combine.

6. Dip each truffle in the white chocolate coating. Return them to the baking sheet and chill in the freezer until firm, about 30 minutes. Store the coated truffles in an airtight container in the freezer for up to 2 months. Let them thaw for a couple of minutes prior to eating.

blueberry "munchkin" muffin bites

Jord and I play this game in which we ask the other person to pick between two similar food items. For example, I will ask him, "Spring rolls or egg rolls?" You have to respond immediately, no hesitations! When he asked me, "Chocolate or glazed munchkin?" I responded with blueberry munchkins. Apparently, they weren't the cool ones and Jord looked at me like I was crazy. But there is no better munchkin than a blueberry munchkin! Who else is with me? I love making these—they satisfy my inner childhood cravings and are the cutest little bites to nosh on! I am counting down the days for when Ezra can eat them with me, too.

MAKES ABOUT 24 MUFFIN BITES

3 tablespoons **liquid coconut oil**, plus more for greasing the muffin cups

1¾ cups **gluten-free oat flour**

1½ teaspoons **baking powder**

½ teaspoon **ground cinnamon**

½ cup **unsweetened nondairy milk**

¼ cup **coconut yogurt**

½ cup **coconut sugar**

1 pasture-raised **egg**

1 teaspoon **pure vanilla extract**

⅔ cup fresh **blueberries**

> **Don't want to use coconut yogurt?** Sub in your favorite thick yogurt alternative. Greek yogurt and almond yogurt both work well!

1. Preheat the oven to 350°F and grease the cups of a 24-cup mini muffin pan with coconut oil.

2. In a large bowl, mix together the oat flour, baking powder, and cinnamon.

3. In a separate large bowl, mix together the nondairy milk, coconut yogurt, coconut sugar, egg, vanilla, and coconut oil until fully combined. Add the dry ingredients to the wet ingredients and mix until just combined (do not overmix).

4. Place the blueberries in a food processor and pulse until they are chopped into small pieces, almost pureed but with some chunks. Fold the blueberries into the batter and stir to combine.

5. Evenly spoon the batter into the mini muffin cups, filling them three-quarters of the way up.

6. Bake until a toothpick inserted in the center of a muffin comes out clean, about 15 minutes. Let the munchkins cool for about 5 minutes before removing them from the muffin pan. Leftover munchkins will keep in an airtight container at room temperature for up to 5 days, or in the freezer for up to 2 months.

mom's **mandel bread**

There is one thing I ask my mom to make for me every single winter: mandel bread, a.k.a. "Jewish biscotti." It is truly the best cookie I have ever eaten in my life (and that's saying a lot). My mom's version is crunchy on the outside, but so soft on the inside and filled with lots of chocolate chips! I'm convinced she puts more in there than she claims because each bite is so perfectly (as in, very!) chocolatey. We have healthified her original recipe to create this gluten- and dairy-free version. I hope you guys love them as much as I do—and don't forget to dip them in some oat milk (see page 48), too!

MAKES ABOUT 20 COOKIES

¾ cup **coconut sugar**

3 large pasture-raised **eggs**

¾ cup **liquid coconut oil**

1 teaspoon **pure vanilla extract**

3 cups **gluten-free oat flour** or sprouted spelt flour

1 teaspoon **baking powder**

⅓ cup **dairy-free dark chocolate chips**

1 teaspoon **ground cinnamon**

1. Preheat the oven to 350°F and line a large baking sheet with parchment paper.

2. In a large bowl, mix together the coconut sugar, eggs, coconut oil, and vanilla until creamy and well combined. Add the oat flour and baking powder, and mix well until the dough comes together. Fold in the dark chocolate chips.

3. Divide the dough in half and form each half into a loaf (10 to 12 inches long and 3 inches wide) on the prepared baking sheet. Sprinkle the loaves with the cinnamon.

4. Bake until the loaves are golden brown, about 30 minutes.

5. Remove the loaves from the oven and slice them into 1-inch-wide cookies. Turn the cookies on their sides on the baking sheet.

6. Return the baking sheet to the oven and bake for 15 minutes. Flip the cookies and bake until they are lightly golden and toasted on each side, about 10 minutes more. Allow the cookies to cool on the baking sheet for a few minutes before serving. Leftover cookies will keep in an airtight container at room temperature for up to 5 days, or in the freezer for up to 2 months. I love these cookies frozen!

mint cacao chip "ice cream"

When I was younger, there were two things I'd get at the ice cream shop: chocolate soft-serve with rainbow sprinkles on a sugar cone (not a waffle cone—only sugar cones over here) or mint chocolate chip ice cream, but only the green kind (see? I am weird). I still love mint chocolate chip ice cream so much that I wanted to make my own vegan version to enjoy at home on the reg. I was beyond impressed with the taste and consistency of this recipe—no frozen bananas needed like in the usual at-home ice cream!

SERVES 4

1 medium **avocado**

1 (13.5-ounce) can **full-fat coconut milk**

⅓ cup **pure maple syrup**

1 tablespoon **pure vanilla extract**

2 teaspoons **peppermint extract**

⅓ cup cold **filtered water**

½ cup **cacao nibs**

1. In a food processor, combine the avocado and coconut milk and pulse to combine. Add the maple syrup, vanilla, peppermint, and cold water, and blend until creamy, about 2 minutes. Pour in the cacao nibs and pulse quickly to incorporate.

2. Transfer the mixture to a medium bowl or a resealable container and freeze for 2 to 3 hours, stirring it every 20 minutes to keep the ice cream from getting too icy. If using a bowl, cover it with plastic wrap.

3. Keep the ice cream in an airtight container in the freezer for up to 2 months. Let it thaw for about 5 minutes before serving.

acknowledgments

I started creating recipes through the ups and the downs and milestones of my twenties. I didn't anticipate that that would be such a roller-coaster of a decade, but it was certainly more delicious and self-evolving than I could ever have imagined. Most people my age still don't know where they want to be in twenty years. Heck, I barely know where I will be in one year! But I do know that when I first began creating my own recipes in a small studio apartment with Jordan (my husband—you probably know him real well by now!), I didn't expect to make a career of it. I just wanted to have my Paleo Chocolate Chip Cookie Cake and eat it, too. And I certainly didn't expect to be sharing all of this with you right here in this book.

I feel as though I am giving the cheesy rehearsed speech you pretend is off-the-cuff when you win an Emmy or an Oscar (like that *Friends* episode with Joey and Rachel at Joey's awards, ha!). But all jokes and cheesiness aside, writing this book has been the ultimate dream. I first set out to write a book about hormones, body image, and pretty much anything besides recipes. That is where

my amazing book agents, Celeste, Sarah, and Anna, came into play. Sarah pretty much told me I was crazy to want to write a book and it *not* be a cookbook: "People want *your* food, Rachel!" So off I went to put together my very first book proposal. And Sarah was right! A cookbook was the right path for me. Thank you so much to the Park & Fine Literary and Media. You guys taught me what a book proposal even *is*, helped me prepare myself for each step of this process, and believed in me since day one (before I even believed this could happen). Thank you for your guidance and support along the way.

Clarkson Potter, I'm still pinching myself that I published my very first cookbook with you. You were the very first publisher I met with, and from the moment I stepped into the conference room for our first meeting, I had the best feeling. I knew if I was going to write a cookbook, *not* partnering with Clarkson Potter wasn't even an option. Thank you for believing in my vision and making my book come to life! Thank you to my amazing and patient editor, Jenn Sit, for bearing with me as a new writer and helping to guide me each step of the way. Thank you to designer Mia Johnson, production editor Terry Deal, Kim Tyner in production, Andrea Portanova and Stephanie Davis in marketing, and publicist Erica Gelbard for all of your incredible work in bringing the book to life.

Aubrie, I still am star struck over having you shoot my first cookbook. As a huge fan of your work for quite some time, it was an honor to have you photograph the dishes for *Just the Good Stuff*. I am so grateful to have gotten to know you and to learn from watching you work your magic with the camera. You made the process seamless, and your calming energy and positives vibes were truly appreciated. I cannot thank you enough for your dedication and time in making each photo absolutely stunning, drool-worthy, and "ooey gooey" as Jenn likes to describe them! Huge thanks to Tatum Magnus, Joshua Goldsmith, Cyd McDowell, Sarah Abrams, Rae Hellard, Kellie Nardin, Maeve Sheridan, Kristen Usui, and Andi McMahon for helping execute the most efficient photo shoot ever!

Thank you, Danielle Daitch, for testing each and every recipe as it moved from my kitchen to yours. You helped to make sure they were as delicious, tasty, and as easy to follow as possible. I am grateful to have found someone who loves to cook and to test healthful recipes as much as I do!

I wouldn't have been able to write this book without my family, the core of my existence and truly my everything. I'm one of those people who are awkwardly close with their parents. I talk to my mom a dozen times a day—she is my rock, my forever best friend, and the first person to taste every single thing I bake (especially anything cinnamon roll-related). I am so grateful for your going totally out of your comfort zone to be photographed for the book, Mama. Thank you for letting me make endless amounts of funfetti cake in our kitchen as a kid to feed my baking addiction from a young age. I'd be lost without my bestie and our daily phone calls and vent sessions. You are the best mama and MeMe in the whole world.

Daddy, you are the strongest human I know (super human, as we like to say). Thank you for teaching me how to hustle and dedicate myself to whatever it is I'm doing. And especially for passing down your epic sweet tooth and oatmeal taste buds. There is no one in this world who appreciates a solid piece of cake or a brownie dipped in a glass of milk more than you do. I will forever fight you for the last piece of mandel bread, though. Or just hide it from you so you don't see it (. . . kidding!).

Seth, my not-so-little little brother: I remember when you tasted one of my recipes for the first time and was shocked at how "tasty" you thought it was. You have come so far in your appreciation of quality food, and I am proud of you for learning how to cook now, too. All my nut-free recipes are forever dedicated to you, and I still believe that one day in the future, you will be able to eat peanut butter cups with me. Until then, we will eat chocolate lava cakes and all the chocolate chip cookie dough ice cream.

My amazing in-laws, Elissa and Glenn, thank you both so much for your unconditional support. Thank you for letting me learn how to cook in your kitchen and for grilling me my favorite wild salmon whenever the craving strikes. I am so grateful to have the most supportive and loving in-laws in my life.

Jordan, my partner in crime: you believed in my vision since day one. As we sat on our couch in our 450-square-foot apartment, you listened to me talk about creating a brand of my own around breakfast and dessert food and never laughed or thought I was crazy. You never question why it takes me forever to photograph my food when we are at lunch or how long it takes me to drizzle the most perfect amount of peanut butter on our pancakes. You still come to the grocery store with me to brainstorm ideas in the aisles and help me carry everything home. You taught me how to slow down a bit and pace myself, something that does not come easily to me. But most of all, thank you for your patience, your kindness, and your love, and for always supporting whatever random idea I have. I know it is a madhouse with our fridge, freezer, and pantry overflowing at all times and having the counter cluttered with four types of brownies. I'm ready for your sweet tooth to come whenever you are (ha!). And most important, thank you for being the best father to Ezra. We are the luckiest to have you. Love you forever, J.

And to my tribe, my Instagram community, my blog readers—you know who you are. I cringe at calling anyone a "follower" because this community is so much more than that. No one is a "follower." You guys are my friends, my family, and are so important to me. Without your support, I wouldn't be here today sharing my recipes in this book. I wouldn't have grown my brand without each and every one of you. I love and appreciate you from the bottom of my heart. Thank you for believing in me and having the enthusiasm to make Classic Dark Chocolate Chip Banana Bread.

index

Note: Page references in *italics* indicate photographs.

Library of Congress Cataloging-in-Publication Data
Names: Mansfield, Rachel, author. | Pick, Aubrie, photographer.
Title: Just the good stuff : 100+ Guilt-Free Recipes to Satisfy All
Your Cravings / Rachel Mansfield ; photographs by Aubrie Pick.
Description: First edition. | New York : Clarkson Potter/Publishers,
an imprint of Random House, a division of Penguin Random
House LLC, [2020] | Includes index.
Identifiers: LCCN 2019000777 (print) | LCCN 2019001082 (ebook)
| ISBN 9781984823373 | ISBN 9781984823366
Subjects: LCSH: Cooking. | Nutrition. | Health. | LCGFT:
Cookbooks.
Classification: LCC TX714 (ebook) | LCC TX714 .M3395 2020
(print) | DDC 641.5—dc23
LC record available at https://lccn.loc.gov/2019000777

ISBN 978-1-9848-2336-6
Ebook ISBN 978-1-9848-2337-3

Printed in China

Book and cover design by Mia Johnson
Illustrations by Mia Johnson
Cover photographs by Aubrie Pick

10 9 8 7 6 5 4 3 2 1

First Edition

"I've always been a fan of Rachel's food philosophy of incorporating real, whole foods into your routine and listening to your body above any other source (of which there can be many in today's world). *Just the Good Stuff* is a beautiful articulation of that philosophy, and it encapsulates recipes that hit on every craving and meal type. It's impossible not to find something you can create on your own and love doing so, regardless of your culinary experience. Rachel's personality and thoughtfulness for her readers shines through each section, making it a useful and entertaining read. As a fellow nut-butter lover, the Peanut Butter Cinnamon Rolls with Coconut Glaze are currently on the top of my 'to-make' list. Yum!"

—**Leigh Keith,** president and cofounder of Perfect Snacks

"Rachel's approach to eating is delicious, mouthwatering, and approachable—and I love that. The recipes in *Just the Good Stuff* are tailored to those looking to indulge without guilt, while also catering to anyone with dietary restrictions. Her recipes are based on various life experiences and learnings, making this book relatable to readers while also making us crave her healthier spin on Crunchy Baked Cinnamon Churro Chips and Homemade Sweet Potato Pierogis."

—**Hannah Bronfman,** author of *Do What Feels Good* and founder of *HBFIT*

"*Just the Good Stuff* is how I want my family to eat. I can make many of these recipes after work in less than thirty minutes—my toddler enjoys eating from this book, too, and the recipes are nutritious enough to eat every day. Rachel has made some of my favorite childhood staples, like nachos made with sweet potato chips and from-scratch marshmallows and graham crackers, just a little bit healthier."

—**Colleen Wachob,** cofounder and co-CEO of *Mindbodygreen*

"*Just the Good Stuff* so perfectly represents Rachel's smart and wholesome approach to food and recipes! This entire book makes my mouth water and my stomach growl, and my entire family is obsessed with her healthier twists on classics like Frosted Blueberry Pastry Tarts and Chocolate Chip Banana Bread. You really can't go wrong with anything in this book!"

—**Melissa Ben-Ishay,** president and chief product officer at Baked by Melissa

"Rachel's recipes are modern, approachable, and simple enough that anyone can make them! *Just the Good Stuff* is a new staple on my bookshelf!"

—**Gina Homolka,** *New York Times* bestselling cookbook author and founder of *Skinnytaste*